H.C.
CHANG

Chinese Literature

VOLUME THREE

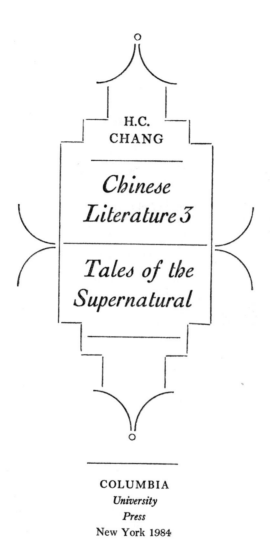

H.C.
CHANG

Chinese
Literature 3

Tales of the
Supernatural

COLUMBIA
University
Press
New York 1984

Library of Congress Cataloging in Publication Data
Main entry under title:
Chinese literature.
  Includes bibliographical references.
  Contents: 2. Nature poetry.   3. Tales of
the supernatural.
  1. Chinese literature—Translations into English.
2. English literature—Translations from Chinese.
I. Chang, H. C. (Hsin-Chang)
PI2658.F1C56 1977   895.1'1'008   81–174030
ISBN 0–231–04288–4 (v. 2)
    0–231–05794–6 (v. 3)

Clothbound editions of Columbia University Press books
are Smyth-sewn.

Foreword

This book, a self-contained study and anthology of Chinese tales of the supernatural, is the third volume of a series on various aspects of Chinese literature.

The series is addressed to the general reading public as well as students of Chinese. It does not offer an assortment of eloquent and moving passages from the whole range of Chinese literature; its aim is to give the Western reader a really close view of certain significant activities on the Chinese literary scene. Thus each volume will be confined to one or two types of writing, and will comprise fresh translations of works or portions of works chosen to illustrate one facet of literary history. A critical survey of its subject will be a feature of each volume.

The plan of the series is as follows:

1. *Popular Fiction and Drama* (*published* 1973)
2. *Nature Poetry* (*published* 1977)
3. *Tales of the Supernatural* (*published* 1983)
4. *Autobiography*
5. *The Vocation of Poetry*
6. *Painting and Poetry*

Contents

General Introduction

1. The Early Supernatural Tale

The supernatural was always part of Chinese life. When making the injunction: 'Show respect towards the gods and the spirits of the departed, but keep aloof from them' (see J. Legge, *The Confucian Analects*, VI.xx), Confucius is presupposing their existence. And in reply to a question on filial piety, the Master says: 'Serve one's parents, when alive, in accordance with ritual; when they die, bury them in accordance with ritual and sacrifice to them in accordance with ritual' (see *The Analects*, II.v.3). Indeed the sacrifice, on anniversary days and at the tomb, *was* for most families until the early decades of this century, a link between the dead, who were presumed to be sentient, and the living.

The ubiquitous grave-mound in the Chinese countryside was, of course, a reminder of death and the hereafter. But there were also the lofty peaks of the mountains, tangible dwelling of the gods, and the liquid surface of the lakes, concealing under their depths a reflected world but indistinctly perceived. Caverns and grottoes awakened expectations of some hidden blessed abode. The crimson and golden clouds at dawn and sunset were part of the pomp of the Emperor or Queen of Heaven's court; a lone white cloud drifting across the sky carried some immortal from one celestial sphere to another; the swiftly changing cloud formations before and after a storm disclosed the shape of an ascending or descending dragon, whose rumbling was the thunder. The moon and the stars painted a silvery heaven, luminous but cold. The black shadows of night and the dim candle flame heightened visions of ghosts and spirits. And the delirious dreams of illness and actual experiences of death and revival made hell and its attendant horrors vivid and real.

Such exercises in fancy, wholly natural, were much encouraged by the mental climate of the Later Han and the ensuing dynasties, during which the country was politically divided for much the greater part of the time and there were recurring wars and widespread confusion. Earlier, Emperor Wu of the Han, and before him, the First Emperor of the Ch'in, had been engrossed in the quest for immortals and the attainment of immortality. But by the Later Han, men's outlook, professedly Confucian, had become permeated with superstitious beliefs deriving from Han cosmology. Even the materialist philosopher Wang Ch'ung (A.D. 27 – ?99), who in such chapters of his *Lun heng* ('Carefully weighed Arguments') as 'Dragons Unreal' (Ssu-pu ts'ung-k'an ed., c. 6), 'On Death' (c. 20), 'On the Falseness of Being after Death' (c. 21) and 'On Apparitions' (c. 22) seeks, though often ineffectually, to offer rational explanations of numerous miraculous events recorded in history, does not always doubt the truthfulness of the accounts, thus tacitly recognizing supernatural phenomena. And the instability and insecurity of men's lives in the third, fourth, fifth and sixth centuries caused them to be ever on the look-out for signs and portents. The search for a haven, safe from danger and exempt from worldly cares, promoted interest and belief in the gods and spirits, in heaven and hell. Many turned to Taoist teaching in the hope of a prolonged existence, others to the Buddhist faith for release from suffering. All were preoccupied with the other world.

The gods of antiquity, as recorded in *Shan-hai ching*

('Treatise on the Mountains and the Seas'; probably 4th–3rd cent. B.C.), were rather like gods in other early societies; they were frightful figures, often animal-shaped or possessing animal features and accompanied by animals or birds, savage and impetuous and unpercipient, associated with some particular locality but also with the natural forces, and of limited powers and influence. But under the patronage of the Emperors, the wizards set up a new type of divinity that took on human attributes and was accessible and attainable— the *hsien*, which is perhaps best rendered 'immortal'. Attainment of the state of immortal was through a strict regimen concluding with the preparation and swallowing of an elixir. According to Ko Hung (283–363), one could become one of three classes of immortals :

> The highest rise bodily into the air and are called 'heavenly immortals'. The intermediate disappear while wandering in the famous mountains and are called 'earthly immortals'. The lowest die, leaving their clothes like the skins of insects, and are called 'immortals with vanishing corpses' (*Pao-p'u-tzu nei-p'ien chiao-shih*, ed. Wang Ming, Chung-hua 1980, c. 2, p.18).

Not all could attain such an exalted plane. The pure, rarefied and ethereal existence of immortals is beyond the reach of most men, and even the few among them chosen to share it cannot enjoy or endure it for long. This incompatibility is reflected in the fourth- and fifth-century tales about love between goddesses and mortals summarized below. In later tales, heaven is often fashioned to the requirements of the earth-bound, as, for instance, in 'Old Chang' (see *infra*, p. 94) from the T'ang. But the best of both worlds, celestial and mundane, is to be had by those successful aspirants, who, assured of immortality, take only a half portion of the elixir so as to enjoy up to a thousand years of earthly life before ascending to heaven (See *Pao-p'u-tzu nei-p'ien chiao-shih*, c. 3, pp. 46–7).

Ghosts are already recorded in the Tso Commentary to

the Annals of Spring and Autumn. In 602 B.C., Tzu-ch'an, in
explaining the apparitions of Po-yu, who had been killed in
battle, maintains:

> When an ordinary man or woman dies a violent death,
> the soul and spirit are still able to keep hanging about
> men in the shape of an evil apparition,

so that a nobleman like Po-yu was all the more capable of
making himself manifest as a ghost (see J. Legge, *The Ch'un
Ts'ew with the Tso Chuen*, Book x, Duke Ch'aou, Year vii,
p. 618, left column). The original attitude towards ghosts
seems to have been a mixture of fear and contempt, as
towards a vicious animal. In the earliest tales, ghosts are
portrayed as malicious beings, to be killed or outmanoeuvred
with tricks. In later tales, ghosts, increasingly associated –
under Buddhist influence – with infernal justice, grow in
stature and might, and are much feared and respected.
Nevertheless, there is a lingering suspicion that ghosts are
inferior to living beings and, indeed, in most tales, ghosts
long to return to life again.

Animal spirits were part of the supernatural world. The
longevity of some species, such as the ape, the tortoise and
the crane, aroused admiration and envy, and animals
generally, with their sense and intelligence and their physical
strength and fitness, exerted a certain fascination, which led
men to attribute magical powers to them. The primitive gods
had the bodies of tigers and dragons, of snakes and birds, of
foxes and pigs. In The Book of Changes, the dragon and the
tiger were held to be in tune with the elements (see R.
Wilhelm, tr. Baynes, *The I Ching*, 1960, p. 8; and 'Introduction' to 'Rain-making', *infra*, p. 76), and this was
endorsed in *Lun heng*, c. 6 'Dragons Unreal', p. 14b. It was
believed that all creatures of great age became spirits that
could take on human shape (see *Lun heng*, c. 22 'Ghosts
Examined', p. 14a). The fox, in particular, was adept at
transformation, especially in later tales; in the early tales,
even the otter, the turtle, the tortoise and the rat transformed

themselves into men and women. In *Pao-p'u-tzu*, the various spirits one may encounter in the mountains are listed, of trees, of metals, of jade, of all kinds of animals, including the tiger, the wolf, the fox, the rabbit, the deer, the dragon, the fish, the crab, the snake, the tortoise, the horse, the cock, the pheasant, the dog, the pig, the rat and the ox; but one may see through the spirits by gazing into a large, bright mirror, which the mountain-dwelling hermit should hang on his back as a protective charm (*Pao-p'u-tzu nei-p'ien chiao-shih*, c.17 'Ascending Mountains', pp. 278 and 274).

In the third century, scholars began to set down unusual occurrences that excited wonder as events worthy in themselves of notice—and not, as previously, as part of history—in short tales forming collections. The tales were often not original compositions, but transcribed or adapted from earlier accounts, and in the majority of instances, the extraordinary happenings relate to the supernatural. And in the fourth, fifth and sixth centuries, further collections of mainly supernatural tales were made. Of these collections, mention may here be made of Kan Pao's *Sou shen chi* ('In Search of the Gods'; 1st half of 4th cent.) and Liu I-ch'ing's *Yu-ming lu* ('Mysteries of the Underworld and this World'; 1st half of 5th cent.). Some of the collections, including *Sou shen chi* and *Yu-ming lu*, survive, though not in their original form and with probably an admixture of later material. Tales from the various collections are included in the Sung compilation of tales, *T'ai-p'ing kuang-chi*, of the tenth century, and other T'ang and Sung compilations. From these and other sources, notably citations in learned works written before the T'ang, Lu Hsün has assembled in his *Ku hsiao-shuo kou-ch'en* ('Relics of Ancient Fiction'; Hsin-i ed. Hongkong 1967) a large number of tales grouped under the titles of the collections to which they originally belonged. And a selection of the best-known is to be found in Hsü Chen-o (ed.), *Han Wei liu-ch'ao hsiao-shuo hsüan* (Ku-tien 1955), hereafter referred to as Hsü, *Selections*. Often the same tale survives in more than one version; also the same tale is sometimes attributed to more than one collection. Thus the authorship of individual tales is not always certain, and in my summaries I have merely indicated, after the title of each tale, the collection from which it is, or is assumed to have been, taken.

Many of the tales deal with immortals. In 'A Jade Goddess from Heaven' (*Sou shen chi*; Hsü, *Selections*, pp. 30–2), a goddess appears to the hero in Changtsing (in Shantung Province) in dreams, and then arrives in a carriage with eight maids to live with him, invisible to his family. After seven or eight years, the parents find a wife for the hero, and the goddess then dwells in a separate room, where she is heard but not seen, but leaves in her carriage when people begin to talk about her. Five years later, on a journey to Loyang (in Honan Province), the hero sees her carriage on the road and joins her. They drive to Loyang together, living for some years as man and wife; subsequently she would visit him on certain days of the year only.

In 'The Snail' (*Sou-shen hou-chi*; 5th cent.; Hsü, *Selections*, pp. 50–1), a poor farmer of Min-hou (in Fukien Province) living alone without relatives, finds a large snail and keeps it in a jar, after which there is always a fire in the hearth and all his meals are prepared. Surprised and bewildered, he returns one morning from the fields and peeps through the fence, to find a young woman emerging from the jar to start work in the kitchen. She, a goddess of the Milky Way, had been sent by heaven as a reward for his virtue, to care for his needs until he could take a wife; but now that he has seen her, she may no longer stay. From then on, the farmer prospers and, shortly afterwards, finds himself a wife.

In 'Liu Ch'en and Yüan Chao' (*Yu-ming lu*; Hsü, *Selections*, pp. 55–6), Liu Ch'en and Yüan Chao of Chenghsien (in Chekiang Province), lost for many days in the Tientai Mountains gathering medicinal herbs, eat some peaches from a hill-top tree and find their hunger allayed. In search of human habitation, they pick up a cup from a stream, and following the stream across a mountain, are greeted by two young women, who claim the cup and take them to a house with a bamboo roof and two ornate beds, where more women arrive, bringing gifts of peaches to congratulate the two on the coming of their husbands. After half a year, it being spring and the birds singing, Liu and Yüan long for home and are sent on their way after a farewell gathering, but they find the village altered and all their relatives and friends gone, save only a descendant of the seventh generation.

In 'Huang Yüan' (*Yu-ming lu*; Hsü, *Selections*, pp. 57–8), Huang Yüan of Taian (in Shantung Province) is led by a dog to a cave inhabited by goddesses and marries one of them, remaining there for a few days. Then, annually on the first of the third month, as agreed, he would fast and purify himself and the carriage of his bride would appear among the clouds.

There are tales about local divinities. In 'Chen Ch'ung' (*Yu-ming lu*; Hsü, *Selections*, pp. 61–2), a local deity outside Mienyang (in Hupeh Province) heading a bridal procession, tries forcibly to marry his daughter to the hero journeying by boat to take up a magistracy near by, who, having already a wife and children, unyieldingly resists the proposal with his drawn sword placed across his knees. And in 'Goddess of the Green River' (*Hsü Ch'i-hsieh chi*; late 5th or early 6th cent.; Hsü, *Selections*, pp. 70–1), the hero singing alone plaintively on an autumn evening in his home in the capital Nanking (in Kiangsu Province), is visited by a lady, who plays on the lute for him and stays for the night. Before dawn, she presents him with a gold hairpin, and he her, a silver bowl and an opaque glass spoon. Visiting the temple of the local river deity the next day, he finds the bowl, the spoon and the lute surrounding a goddess and her maid in the likeness of his late visitors.

A great many of the tales are about ghosts. In 'Sun O' (*Lieh i chuan*; 3rd cent.; Hsü, *Selections*, pp. 25–6), the ghost

of a dead son smarting under his burden as infernal runner of
the Tai-shan district (in Shantung Province) appears to his
mother in a dream to ask his father to recommend him to the
principal singer of the Memorial Temple, who is about to
become infernal Magistrate of the Tai-shan district. The
principal singer, after promising to promote the ghost son,
expires. In 'Ch'in Chü-po' (*Sou shen chi*; Hsü, *Selections*,
p. 35), an old man of Lang-yeh (part of Shantung Province)
walking alone in the night while intoxicated, is accosted and
beaten up by two ghosts pretending to be his grandsons. A
few nights later, they molest him again. Bent on revenge,
he then goes walking with a sharp knife, feigning drunkenness. When his anxious grandsons come out in the dark
to meet him, mistaking them for ghosts, he kills them
both.

In 'The King of Wu's Daughter' (*Sou shen chi*; Hsü,
Selections, pp. 39–40), Yü, the King of Wu's daughter, who
has secretly promised to marry the student Han Chung, dies
of despair when the King rejects the suit brought forward on
his behalf by his parents. Returning from his travels three
years later, Han weeps at Yü's tomb in Soochow (in Kiangsu
Province) and her ghost comes forward; at her invitation
he enters the tomb with her, leaving on the fourth day after
receiving from her a large pearl as parting gift. When the
King accuses Han of rifling the tomb, Yü appears to defend
him; her mother then embracing Yü, finds her to be like a
wisp of smoke. In 'Lu Ch'ung' (*Sou shen chi*; Hsü, *Selections*,
pp. 41–3), the hero chasing after a roebuck outside Chohsien
(in Hopeh Province), is received into the tomb of Prefect
Ts'ui and marries the Prefect's daughter, remaining with her
for three days before being sent back in an ox-drawn cart.
Four years later, disporting himself by the river on the third
of the third month in accordance with custom, he sees an
ox-drawn cart on the bank with his wife and a three-year-old
boy in it. She has come to present his son to him, and leaves
him with a poem and a gold bowl, later found to be one

placed in the Prefect's daughter's coffin by relatives. The boy, an object of suspicion at first, grows up and thrives.

In 'Chi K'ang' (*Ling-kuai chih*; prob. 2nd half of 4th cent.; Hsü, *Selections*, pp. 45–6), the poet and philosopher Chi K'ang spending the night alone in a rest-house some distance from Loyang, plays on the guitar and is applauded by the voice of the ghost of one who had suffered decapitation. At Chi's entreaty the ghost appears, propping up its head with its hand, and after playing a few pieces on the guitar, teaches Chi the authentic version of the suite 'Kuang-ling san'.

In 'The New Ghost' (*Yu-ming lu*; Hsü, *Selections*, pp. 66–7), an old ghost teaches a new ghost how to obtain food offerings by frightening the populace with mischievous tricks. In 'Hsü T'ieh-chiu' (*Yüan-hun chih*; 2nd half of 6th cent.; Hsü, *Selections*, pp. 80–1), a step-mother in Lienshui (in Kiangsu Province) who calls her own son 'Pestle' and maltreats her step-son Mortar, eventually beats Mortar to death. Mortar's ghost presently returns to haunt her and to torment the half-brother Pestle until, a month later, Pestle dies of illness.

In 'Hung' (*Yüan-hun chih*; Hsü, *Selections*, p. 82), the merchant Hung is put to death by a port official near Yoyang (in Hunan Province) on a false accusation and his raft, several hundred feet in length and made of the best timber, confiscated to provide material for a temple to be erected over the late Emperor's tomb. Before his execution, Hung asks his family to place paper, ink and writing brush in his coffin to enable him to file a suit in hell against the official, who, a month later, sees Hung's ghost coming towards him and dies, vomiting blood. Within a year, all concerned in perpetrating the injustice die; and the temple is razed to the ground by fire immediately after completion.

Of numerous accounts of visits to hell, 'Chao T'ai' (*Ming-hsiang chi*; 2nd half of 5th cent.; Hsü, *Selections*, pp. 73–5) is the outstanding example. Chao T'ai, a scholar and man of virtue of Tsingho (in Hopeh Province), dies at

B

the age of thirty-five and revives ten days later. After death, Chao is escorted to a large city with dark walls the colour of pewter. His name is recorded by clerks clad in black and checked against a ledger by a judge, after which he is questioned in another hall by an official in crimson robes and made an overseer of two thousand labourers repairing an embankment. He is then appointed Inspector of the Infernal Prisons and visits the various torture chambers complete with gridiron, red-hot bronze pillar, boiling cauldron and tree of swords, filled with hundreds of prisoners, naked and bleeding from open gashes, or scorched, or mangled, or mutilated. He learns that, from these prisons, some are released through Buddhist faith and delivered to an adjoining House for the Blessed. He also visits the City of Transformation, in which the wicked turn into beasts. An official-in-charge then decides that Chao has been called before his time and sends him home, and Chao and his family become devout Buddhists.

'Wang Tao-p'ing' (*Sou shen chi*, ed. Hu Huai-ch'en, Commercial Press 1957, c.15, pp. 108–9) is a good example of the tale about revival after death. Wang Tao-p'ing, after a long absence in the south, returns to Changan (in Shensi Province) to learn that his beloved, Fu-yü, had been married against her will to someone else and had died three years later, heart-broken. At her grave he calls her name thrice and reminds her of their exchanged vows, whereupon her ghost appears, protesting her innocence and telling him that her body is still whole and that, if he should exhume her, she would revive. He then opens the grave and, finding her alive, returns home with her.

Immortals and ghosts are but projections of men and women, and an idealization of the human scene. Animal spirits, to figure so prominently in T'ang and still later tales, are less easily woven into a story, and there are fewer interesting early tales about them. In 'The Sick Dragon' (*Sou shen chi*, ed. Hu, c. 20, p.151) a farmer praying for rain outside a dragon's cave in the Prefecture of Wei (in Honan Province), is answered with a shower, but the rain-water proving foul and stinking, the sage Sun Teng declares that the dragon is ill and its rain of no avail to the crops. Thereupon the dragon, who has an ulcer on its back, appears in the guise of an old man to be cured by Sun and rewards the local inhabitants by causing a downpour, during which a rock cracks to reveal a well underneath.

In 'The Purple One' (*Sou shen chi*, ed. Hu, c.18, pp.140–1), Wang Ling-hsiao, an officer serving under the Prefectural Commander of Hsi-hai (i.e. the eastern part of Tsinghai Province), is reported missing for a second time. The Commander suspecting that Wang has been snatched away by some evil spirit, leads foot and mounted soldiers and hounds in a search and finds him in an empty tomb outside the town, the evil spirit—a fox—having fled at the noise of men and dogs. When taken home, Wang is discovered to be already somewhat like a fox in appearance, not responding to the advances of his companions but repeatedly calling for his fox mate, 'The Purple One'. After over ten days, having regained his reason, Wang reveals that the fox would at first appear as a beautiful woman in some corner of the house or near the hen-coop beckoning to him and that he would then follow her to her lair, where he was blissfully happy. 'The Purple One' was the name of a wanton woman of ancient times who turned into a fox.

In 'Lü Ssu' (*Ch'i-hsieh chi*; 5th cent.; *Ku hsiao-shuo kou-ch'en*, pp.235–6), Lü Ssu spending the night with a young woman at a rest-house outside a temple beside a hill, loses sight of her and sets out in pursuit. In the dark he comes upon an imposing official residence, in which a silk-hatted official seated at his desk is being attacked, as in some game, by a large crowd of followers. Drawing his sword against them, Lü kills all he can lay hands on and finds over a hundred dead foxes in a large tomb, from which he rescues his crazed woman companion and scores of other women, some already half-transformed into foxes, who are claimed by their families.

In 'The Fox that sought shelter' (*Yu-ming lu*; *Ku hsiao-shuo kou-ch'en*, p. 269) a woman with a child in her arms seeking shelter in a mountain hut and falling asleep by the fire, changes into a fox clutching a black hen, and a man who calls on the following day to ask about his wife also turns into a fox when beset by a dog. And in 'The Fox in the Tomb' (*Hsi-ching tsa-chi*; prob. 6th cent.; Hsü, *Selections*, p. 90), the Prince of Kuang-ch'uan excavating the tomb of Luan Shu, a Minister of Chin in the Chou dynasty, comes across a white fox, which is wounded in one of its left feet by his followers. The same night, a man with thick white hair and whiskers appears reproachfully in a dream to the Prince and strikes the Prince's left foot with a stick, resulting, on waking, in a sore that lasts until his dying day.

In 'Chang Fen' (*Lieh i chuan*; Hsü, *Selections*, p. 27), an early tale about inanimate objects, the new owner of a haunted house discovers the three hatted figures whom he sees in the hall at night, clothed respectively in yellow, green and white, to be three separate hoards of gold, copper cash and silver, buried in the courtyard, and their invisible interlocutor, a pestle under the cooking stove.

The early supernatural tale is seriously deficient in narrative art. The characters are shadowy, the events wanting in verisimilitude. The story is often thin, and only the bare bones are given, and that not always clearly, in part because of the imperfect state of existing versions. Accepting the marvellous as fact and addressing a captive audience, the writers assumed that the mere mention of gods and spirits would impress and were seldom concerned to impart a supernatural experience. And indeed, from the evidence of the more unsatisfactory examples, the writers were often trying to fashion a tale out of two or more unrelated occurrences, not necessarily supernatural. Nevertheless, the better tales already possess some degree of unity; there is fairly skilled use of dialogue; and the narrative is sometimes embellished with gracefully unobtrusive verse. Slowly and awkwardly the supernatural tale was taking shape.

In this General Introduction I have tried to trace the development of the supernatural tale from the simple sketches at about the time of the Three Kingdoms to the rounded and animated representations in the celebrated *Ch'uan-ch'i* tale of the T'ang and thence on to the pale imitations of the Sung and the accomplished, but largely derivative, products of the Ming, from the third to the fifteenth century. A separate Introduction is made below to the seventeenth-century collection *Liao-chai chih-i*, which marks a fresh beginning and which is also the culmination of the supernatural tale. In the General Introduction I have presented, in the form of summaries, some of the more interesting tales from the various periods: Wei and Chin and the Southern Dynasties (3rd – 6th cent.); T'ang (7th – 9th cent.); Sung (10th – 13th cent.); early and middle Ming (14th – 15th cent.). And in the Introductions to individual tales I have summarized and discussed similar tales that may help to explain the tale in question; for the first seven tales, from the T'ang, I have relied, for the most part, on examples to be found in *T'ai-p'ing kuang-chi*, a distinction being made between those tales written before the T'ang, which are given the epithet 'early', and tales from the T'ang and the tenth century. It has not been my endeavour to trace the origin, or chart the prevalence, of ideas and beliefs, though in the fuller summaries I have usually indicated the locality in which a tale is set. Certainly the tales cited and discussed need not be the earliest to deal with the core of the story; early accounts are apt to be preceded by still earlier ones, sometimes in philosophical treatises or works of history, and a later instance may be just as significant as an early one. Thus regarding the whole course of the supernatural tale from the period of the Three Kingdoms to the Ming as one unbroken tradition, I have preferred, on the whole, to let the tales, earlier and later, supply each other's commentary.

2. THE T'ANG CH'UAN-CH'I TALE

The supernatural figures prominently in the rise of a new
literary form in the T'ang, the *Ch'uan-ch'i* tale, literally, 'a
tale transmitting the marvellous'. Whereas earlier writers
had been concerned merely to record miracles and wonders,
the T'ang writers were intent on telling a tale, on enlivening
it with characters in a setting with some semblance of
actuality, on adorning it with ingenious and elegant phrases,
and on projecting their own ideals into the course of the
action, thereby identifying themselves with hero and heroine
and their adventures and exploits. Although the writers of
the *Ch'uan-ch'i* tale inherited four centuries of burning
curiosity about spiritual manifestations and a large body of
supernatural lore, their interest in the world of the spirits
was really more literary than pious. They were also actuated
by the motive of display, in that their tales were often
submitted to intending patrons for perusal and approval, as
vehicles of the writers' talents in prose, in poetry, in narrative
and in moral reflections. And, indeed, for the telling of a tale,
there is no better subject than the marvellous and supernatural, which constitute the theme of half of the *Ch'uan-ch'i*
tales, the other favourite subject being love, which is
sometimes combined with the supernatural in treatment.

Apart from heightened narrative skill, the *Ch'uan-ch'i* tale
is characterised by the flamboyant and naive outlook of its
writers. The flamboyance manifests itself in the ostentatious
tone, the zestful narrative, the rich descriptions, the florid
style and the luxuriant language. As regards naivety, the
world is seen through the starry eyes of youth and innocence,
which enables the writers to enter readily into scenes of
enchantment, mundane or supernatural. The supernatural is
indeed accepted as part of the wonders of existence without
question or explanation. Resulting from a fusion of this
flamboyance and naivety, the T'ang imagination may be

likened to the spectrum of a rainbow lending colour and magic to even the plain and ordinary.

The characters portrayed in the *Ch'uan-ch'i* tales are equally flamboyant and naive. The T'ang was an era in which scholars were not yet weak and helpless, nor ladies, stilted patterns of virtue. In the tales, the men are full-blooded and manly, abounding with energy and gusto, and extravagant in speech and behaviour. The tales, too, depict a world in which men and women engage spontaneously in social activity, far more readily than in later times and with far fewer scruples and inhibitions: they play music and dance, they ride and hunt, they exchange verses extempore, they flirt and love, all without the least trace of self-consciousness. Every man is a hero out to conquer, every woman a goddess, every residence a charmed palace. And the supernatural is but an extension of this enchantment for the artless hero, who is not so much credulous as easily wonder-struck.

The *Ch'uan-ch'i* tales were, in the seventh and eighth centuries, individual compositions that circulated among friends, but perhaps in response to the growing demand of readers, whole collections of tales by a single author began to appear in the ninth century. Of these, the best known are: Niu Seng-ju's *Hsüan-kuai lu* ('Tales about the Mysterious and Strange'), Li Fu-yen's imitation of it, *Hsü Hsüan-kuai lu* ('More Tales about the Mysterious and Strange'), both of the first half of the ninth century, and P'ei Hsing's *Ch'uan-ch'i* ('Tales about the Marvellous'), of the second half of the ninth century, from whose title the whole genre has acquired its name. But few of the ninth century collections survive intact, and the chief source for the T'ang supernatural tale is the monumental Sung compilation *T'ai-p'ing kuang-chi* (completed 978; Jen-min ed. in 5 vols. 1959), a collection of tales and anecdotes from the Han to the early Sung in 500 *chüan* dealing with subjects ranging from immortals, Taoists and Buddhists to dreams, magic, ghosts, dragons, tigers, apes and foxes. Of modern collections of *T'ang ch'uan-ch'i* tales, including supernatural tales, Wang P'i-chiang (ed.), *T'ang-jen hsiao-shuo* (Ku-tien 1955) is indispensable, and I have used it for the translations of the seven T'ang tales in this volume; Lu Hsün (ed.), *T'ang Sung ch'uan-ch'i chi* (Wen-hsüeh ku-chi 1955) and Chang Yu-ho (ed.), *T'ang Sung ch'uan-ch'i hsüan* (Jen-min, 2nd printing 1979) are both valuable.

In what may be regarded as the earliest *Ch'uan-ch'i* tale, Wang Tu's 'The Ancient Mirror' (c. 620; *T'ang-jen hsiao-shuo*, pp. 3 – 9), an ancient mirror, carried in turn by two brothers on their travels, unmasks and kills various animal spirits it shines upon, including a fox, a snake, a tortoise, an ape, a dragon, a cock, a weasel, a rat and a gecko. Some of these animal spirits are the subject of other T'ang tales.

In the anonymous 'The White Ape' (1st half of 7th cent.; *T'ang-jen hsiao-shuo*, pp. 15 – 17), an ape spirit is tracked to its cave deep in the wild and steep mountains of Kwangsi Province, in which it holds captive thirty beautiful women, by the husband of one of them, and killed with the connivance of the captives. Li Kung-tso's 'An Ancient Treatise on Mountains and Rivers' (c. 814; *T'ang Sung ch'uan-ch'i chi*, pp. 79 – 81) contains a description of a submerged deity of the Huai river in the shape of a gigantic ape chained to the foot of Tortoise Hill at Chuyi (in Kiangsu Province).

In P'ei Hsing's 'Sun K'o' (2nd half of 9th cent.; *T'ang-jen hsiao-shuo*, pp. 279 – 82), an ape brought to Loyang from a monastery near Kaoyao (in Kwangtung Province) transforms herself into a Miss Yüan ('Ape'), a rich heiress, and marries the hero, bearing him two sons. On a journey to the south with her husband and children, Miss Yüan insists on visiting the monastery, where at the sight of scores of apes screaming and jumping among the pine trees, she tears off her clothes and resumes the shape of an ape, disappearing with the other apes into the mountains.

In Shen Chi-chi's 'Miss Jen' (781; see *infra*, p. 45), a fox spirit in the capital Ch'ang-an (i.e. Sian in Shensi Province) is made convincingly human; the tale is episodic and draws on earlier fox lore, but has had much influence on later tales about foxes. In Huang-fu Mei's 'Wang Chih-ku' (last quarter of 9th cent.; *T'ang-jen hsiao-shuo*, pp. 289–92), the hero, separated from a hunting party outside Loyang, is received into a household of foxes, who propose marrying their daughter to him until they learn with horror that he is a protégé of the notorious hunter, General Chang Chih-fang, when they rudely expel him. The general, learning of the hero's adventures on the following day, asks to be led with his huntsmen to the same spot, where they find a dozen or so large tombs, infested with foxes. Driven out by spades and fumes, the foxes are rounded up and killed.

In Li Ch'ao-wei's 'Liu I' (late 8th cent.; *T'ang-jen hsiao-shuo*, pp. 62–8), a tale about dragons, Liu I meets near Kingyang (in Shensi Province) a bedraggled young woman, who is the daughter of the Dragon King of Tungting Lake (in Hunan Province) and who has been reduced to severe distress by the unkind treatment of her wayward husband and cruel parents-in-law. Liu undertakes to carry a letter for her to her father, being about to return to his home near the lake. In the Dragon King's palace, the news brought by Liu spreads dismay. In a fit of rage, the King's brother rushes to Kingyang to wreak havoc, kills and eats up the dragon husband, and brings the King's daughter back to her father. Liu is feasted and entertained with music and dancing, but firmly declines when the dragon uncle tries to compel him to marry the niece. Liu returns home, loaded with gifts of exotic pearls and gems, and eventually marries a beautiful widow, who turns out to be the Dragon King's daughter, with whom he leads the existence of an immortal.

In the anonymous 'Efficacious Dragon Deities' (late 9th cent.; *T'ang Sung ch'uan-ch'i chi*, pp. 188–200), a dragon widow near Kingchwan (in Kansu Province), who claims to be related to the dragons in the tale of 'Liu I', invokes the help of the local commander in resisting the phantom army of a dragon suitor. And in Shen Ya-chih's 'Plaintive Verses from the South' (818; *T'ang-jen hsiao-shuo*, pp. 157–8), a girl whom the hero finds weeping under the bridge over the Lo river in Loyang, is in the habit of chanting plaintive verses in the style of the ancient anthology of songs from the south, *Ch'u tz'u*. After several years, she leaves him to return as a dragon to Tungting Lake, where, over a dozen years later, he sees her dancing and singing in the company of numerous musicians in quaint dress on a large decorated boat.

In the anonymous 'Cheng Te-lin' (1st half of 9th cent.; *T'ang-jen hsiao-shuo*, pp. 187–9), the god of Tungting Lake is not specified as a dragon. Cheng Te-lin, Police Officer of Siangtan (in Hunan Province), frequently travels by boat to Wuchang (in Hupeh Province) to visit relatives. Crossing Tungting Lake, he would meet the boat of an old water-chestnut seller, with whom he would share his pine-bark wine. On a return journey from Wuchang, attracted by a girl in a salt merchant's large boat, he throws on to her fishing hook a silk handkerchief on which he has inscribed a poem, and she ties it round her wrist. The wind then rising, the large boat surges ahead and is later reported lost in the lake. Cheng writes a poem mourning the fair one on the river and throws it into the lake. The god of the lake, who is none other than the water-chestnut seller, reads the poem and orders the girl's body to be released near Cheng's boat, whereupon she is rescued and marries Cheng. On another journey several years later, she meets the god again, disguised as a boatman, and receives his permission for her boat to visit the under-water world, in which her drowned parents have their own dwelling.

In Hsüeh Yung-jo's 'Wei Yu' (1st half of 9th cent.; *T'ang-jen hsiao-shuo*, pp. 253–4), a zither string coiled round a reed in the river at Wenchow (in Chekiang Province) turns out to be a white dragon, a thousand feet in length. And in Yüan Chiao's 'T'ao Hsien' (868; *T'ang-jen hsiao-shuo*, pp. 256–7), the hero, a descendant of the poet and recluse

T'ao Yüan-ming and an inveterate wanderer in search of beautiful scenery, would amuse himself with his three prize possessions, an ancient sword, a jade bracelet and a blackamoor slave who is a former sailor and diver, by throwing the sword and bracelet into the river and asking the slave to retrieve them. Eventually, the slave is killed by a dragon in the still and black waters of a section of the Yangtze under Western Fort (i.e. Hsi-sai-shan in Hupeh Province).

In Li Fu-yen's 'Rain-making' (1st half of 9th cent.; see *infra*, p. 79), the hero, Li Ching, makes a brief sojourn in a dragons' palace in the Huo Mountains (in Shansi Province) and is entrusted with the task of making rain. But the actual rain-making is somewhat perfunctory, so that the tale never becomes really animated. The hero also seems deficient in charm despite the villagers', and the dragons', high estimation of him.

In Niu Seng-ju's 'Kuo Yüan-chen' (1st half of 9th cent.; *T'ang-jen hsiao-shuo*, pp. 212–14), the hero cuts off a hand of the 'Black General', a deity to whom the villagers of Fenyang (in Shansi Province) offer annually a young girl as bride, and finds this to be a trotter, whereupon he tracks the bleeding pig to its lair, where, surrounded by the villagers, it is killed.

In the anonymous 'Goblins in the Night at a Tung-yang Temple' (prob. 2nd half of 9th cent.; *T'ang Sung ch'uan-ch'i chi*, pp. 176–88), the hero, Ch'eng Tzu-hsü, comes across, in a deserted temple east of Weinan (in Shensi Province), a camel, an ass, an ox, a dog, a cock, a cat and two hedgehogs, who converse in the dark and recite verses revealing their identity. The hero's name Ch'eng Tzu-hsü ('Entirely Fictitious') echoes the title of Niu Seng-ju's tale 'Yüan Wu-yu' ('It did not happen'; 1st half of 9th cent.; *T'ang-jen hsiao-shuo*, pp. 197–8), a tale about inanimate objects that come to life, of which the anonymous tale is an imitation. In Niu's tale, the hero, Yüan Wu-yu, spends the night in a deserted farmhouse outside Yangchow (in Kiangsu Province)

and overhears four strange figures chatting and declaiming
verses about themselves under the moon. In the morning, he
finds a washerwoman's club, a lampstand, a water bucket and
a broken pot. In Niu's tale 'Ts'en Shun' (1st half of 9th cent.;
T'ang-jen hsiao-shuo, pp. 207 – 8), the hero living alone in a
mountain cottage (in Shan-hsien, i.e. Sanmenhsia in Honan
Province) built over an ancient tomb complete with a
chamber full of funerary objects including scores of suits of
armour and a bronze chess set, is invited to join in the
campaigns of the armies of two rival kingdoms night after
night. And in P'ei Hsing's 'Lu Han' (2nd half of 9th cent.;
T'ai-p'ing kuang-chi, c. 372, pp. 2956 – 7), a two-feet-high
funerary figure of a servant girl in a forest outside Loyang
offers the hero a drink made from the blood of a large black
snake.

In Li Fu-yen's 'The Tiger' (1st half of 9th cent.; see *infra*,
pp. 87 – 9), a momentary impulse transforms a gentle scholar
into a man-eating tiger for a night and a day. The wonder is
recounted with a simplicity that conveys something of the
experience of the transformation itself and of the sensation
of being a tiger. And in Li's 'The Carp' (1st half of 9th cent.;
see *infra*, pp. 71 – 5), the transformation of the hero into a
carp also seems entirely natural and convincing, though the
tale is somewhat spoilt by the implied moral; and the
blow-by-blow account of the course of events in proof of the
hero's veracity is a little tedious.

Chang Chuo's 'A Visit to the Cave of Some Goddesses'
(late 7th cent.; *T'ang-jen hsiao-shuo*, pp. 19 – 33) may perhaps
claim to be the earliest *Ch'uan-ch'i* tale about immortals.
The hero, who is the author himself, climbs up a precipice in
a ravine in the Chi-shih Mountains (in Kansu Province) in
search of a cave inhabited by immortals and is given shelter
and entertainment in a mansion of the utmost magnificence
by two transcendently beautiful ladies. The hero woos both
ladies with witty compliments and verses, to which they
respond in kind, and one of them grants him her favours

before he departs at dawn on his official mission. As in 'The White Ape', the setting, in wild nature, is unearthly and may have suggested, in the first instance, the idea of the supernatural, though the title is no more than a figure of speech, part of the love convention of literature.

In Niu Seng-ju's 'The Student Ts'ui' (1st half of 9th cent.; *T'ang-jen hsiao-shuo*, pp. 196–7), the student Ts'ui tending the flowers of noble strain in his garden at the mouth of a ravine, is surprised by the sight of a passing lady on horseback on her way into the ravine with her maids. When the procession is repeated on the following mornings, Ts'ui tries to induce the lady to stay, and eventually an old woman servant gives consent, on behalf of the lady, to marrying him. Ts'ui's mother being in failing health, suspects the daughter-in-law—more beautiful than any she has seen among statues or in pictures—to be a fox. Deeply offended, the lady, who is the third daughter of the Queen Mother of Heaven, departs for her sister's home in the ravine, leaving, as parting gift for Ts'ui, a white jade box.

In P'ei Hsing's 'P'ei Hang' (2nd half of 9th cent.; *T'ang-jen hsiao-shuo*, pp. 272–5), the hero woos, on a boat journey on the Han river (in Hupeh Province), a coldly beautiful lady, who leaves him with a poem with a cryptic reference to Lan-ch'iao. At Lan-ch'iao (near Lantien in Shensi Province), which he reaches when continuing his journey on horseback, he is given a drink at a roadside cottage by an old woman and her dazzlingly beautiful granddaughter. The woman promises the hand of her granddaughter, Yün-ying, on condition that the hero comes back with a jade pestle for her to pound some divine medicine. The hero returns with the jade pestle and helps to compound the medicine. Scores of immortals attend the wedding, including the lady on the boat, who is the elder sister of the bride. The hero and his wife live for ever afterwards in a cave for immortals.

In Huang-fu Mei's 'Prefect Wen' (late 9th cent.; *T'ang Sung ch'uan-ch'i hsüan*, pp. 184–5), an old and ragged Taoist

priest, flogged for interrupting the procession of the Prefect
of Ch'ang-an the capital, turns out, when followed to his
home, to be an immortal. When the contrite Prefect himself
comes to the door to ask for pardon, the Taoist agrees to
spare the man's family but offers no remission for the
Prefect himself, whose numerous misdeeds soon bring about
his own death.

And in Hsüeh Yung-jo's 'Hsü Tso-ch'ing' (1st half of 9th
cent.; *T'ang-jen hsiao-shuo*, pp. 246–7), a Taoist—a near
immortal—who frequently visits a temple outside Chenglu
(in Szechwan Province), is hit, in the shape of a crane in
flight over a sandy moor to the east of the Capital Ch'ang-an,
by an arrow from the bow of the Brilliant Emperor, and
leaves the arrow on the wall of the temple, to be picked up
years later by the Emperor fleeing from the rebels in the
north.

In Niu Seng-ju's 'Chang Tso' (1st half of 9th cent.;
T'ang-jen hsiao-shuo, pp. 204–7), a man riding on a black
donkey with white hooves outside Huhsien (in Shensi
Province) claiming to be over two hundred years old,
attributes his longevity to Taoist observances he practised
in his previous reincarnation, in which he was rewarded with
a prolonged visit to an enchanted land, entered through the
ear of one of a pair of mysterious celestial visitors. And in
P'ei Hsing's 'T'ao and Yin' (2nd half of 9th cent.; *T'ang-jen
hsiao-shuo*, pp. 284–6), two old men, gatherers of pine resin
and the roots of firs, drinking in a pine forest, are joined by
a man and a woman from the reign of the First Emperor of
the Ch'in dynasty, who relate their history, having attained
immortality by feeding on fir-cones and pine syrup, and
banishing earthly thoughts (see the account of the Ch'in
palace lady leaping across gullies and ravines under Chung-
nan Mountain in *Pao-p'u-tzu nei-p'ien chiao-shih*, c.11, p.188,
for the probable source of this tale).

In Li Fu-yen's 'Yang Kung-cheng' (1st half of 9th cent.;
T'ang-jen hsiao-shuo, pp. 215–7), a village woman of Wensiang

(in Honan Province), diligent at her tasks but of a quiet and meditative disposition, is chosen to be an immortal and installed in a ceremony on Yün-t'ai Peak on Hwa-shan (in Shensi Province). And in Li's 'Old Chang' (1st half of 9th cent.; see *infra*, pp. 94–100), Chang, an old gardener of Liuho (in Kiangsu Province), marries a retired official's daughter and takes her away to their celestial home. It contains a completely mundane picture of heaven, its *nouveau riche* ostentatious vulgarity relieved only towards the end by Chang's producing a straw hat from humbler days.

Many of the T'ang tales are about ghosts. Li Ching-liang's 'Li Chang-wu' (early 9th cent.; *T'ang-jen hsiao-shuo*, pp. 56–8) captures something of the spiritual manifestation of deep and intense longings and offers a ghostly experience: During over a month's stay at a lodging-house in Hwahsien (in Shensi Province), Li Chang-wu becomes the lover of the landlord's daughter-in-law. Eight years later, he visits her again but finds the house deserted, and a neighbour informs him that she had died pining for him, and that her last wish had been for him to stay again in the house so that they could meet in spirit. At the second watch that night in his room, the lamp flickers several times and creeping noises from a dark corner gather shape as a woman. It is she, dressed in her former clothes, though swifter and more nervous in movement, and softer and higher-pitched in her voice. They embrace as if they had never been parted, and send the servants repeatedly to see if the morning star is out. At the fifth watch, they rise from their bed to look at the stars in the Milky Way, and she presents him with a piece of divine jade and a poem before disappearing into a corner. He leaves for his destination, but on his journey back to the capital, hears her voice in the air bidding him for ever farewell.

In Ch'en Hsüan-yu's 'Twixt Soul and Body' (c.780; see *infra*, pp. 59–61), which is not about a ghost, a girl's longing for her beloved leads her soul to join him on his journey, leaving her body behind in her parents' home in Hengyang (in Hunan Province). Five years later, he returns there, and soul and body are reunited.

In the anonymous 'Music from the World of the Shades' (2nd half of 9th cent.; *T'ang-jen hsiao-shuo*, pp.190−1), an aunt, a highly gifted musician, returns from the world of the dead to teach her two nieces ten pieces for the zither currently performed in infernal palaces. The nieces play with their eyes shut, and the aunt's voice is heard, but whether she appears is left in doubt by the narrator. In Li Kung-tso's 'The Beldame Feng' (811; see *infra*, pp.64−6), in which the dead are portrayed as intensely involved with the living, the ghost of the wife of the Assistant Magistrate of Tung-cheng (in Anhwei Province) appears, weeping despondently, to the old woman Feng on the eve of his remarriage.

In Niu Seng-ju's 'Prefect Ch'i's Daughter' (1st half of 9th cent.; *T'ang-jen hsiao-shuo*, pp.209−11), Mrs Li, the married daughter of Prefect Ch'i of Jaochow (i.e. Poyang in Kiangsi Province), is threatened and later killed by the ghost of a former owner of the Prefect's house, the Han Prince Wu Jui; who objects to the pollution of childbirth. At the earnest entreaty of her husband Li, an old village teacher, who is an immortal in disguise, arrests and tries the angry ghost, pronouncing it guilty of murder. The old man also brings about the resurrection of the lady (whose body has decayed) by rolling eight women ghosts of Mrs Li's type in appearance into one and smearing a thick coat of glue over the resultant body.

Indeed, ghosts from history figure in a number of the tales. Ch'en Hung's 'The Everlasting Remorse' (807; *T'ang-jen hsiao-shuo*, pp.117−9), written as an introduction to Po Chü-i's poem on the same subject, recounts the well-known story of the Brilliant Emperor and his Precious Consort. A Taoist searching, at the Emperor's behest, through the heavens and the underworld for the spirit of the Precious Consort, finally lights upon her dwelling on an island inhabited by immortals. She receives him and asks him to return half of a gold hairpin and part of a jewellery box, which had been the Emperor's first gifts to her, to His Majesty in token of her devotion. She also reveals a vow once made by the Emperor when alone with her on the seventh of the seventh month, the night of the reunion in heaven of the two stars, the Weaving Maid and the Herd Boy, that in every reincarnation to come, he and she would be husband and wife.

In the anonymous 'A Journey through Chou and Ch'in' (1st half of 9th cent.; *T'ang-jen hsiao-shuo*, pp.151–3), the hero Niu Seng-ju is given shelter in the tomb of an Empress of the Han dynasty south of Loyang and meets the ghosts of various Imperial Concubines, including that of the Brilliant Emperor's Precious Consort, spending the night with one of them. The piece seems to have been written to discredit the Minister Niu Seng-ju (779–847), author of a whole collection of *Ch'uan-ch'i* tales (see *supra*, p.14), who appears in this tale as both hero and story-writer. In P'ei Hsing's 'Ts'ui Wei' (2nd half of 9th cent.; *T'ang-jen hsiao-shuo*, pp.275–9), the hero, possessed of some magical healing mugwort, falls into a pit outside Canton (in Kwangtung Province) inhabited by a white dragon and removes the tumour on the dragon's lip, whereupon the dragon carries him on its back through a subterranean passage to the tomb of Chao T'o, Prince of Southern Yüeh in the Han. The hero's father had, some years previously, written a poem lamenting the decay of Prince of Southern Yüeh's Tower, which had induced the Prefect of the time to restore the monument as one of the local sights. In gratitude, the ghost of the Prince now sends the son home with a fabulous pearl from Arabia and one of the Prince's ghost concubines as wife.

And in two of Shen Ya-chih's tales, ghostly figures of the past appear in dreams: In 'A Strange Dream' (815; *T'ang-jen hsiao-shuo*, pp.160–1), the owner of an old house in the capital Ch'ang-an sees in a dream a beautiful woman in ancient dress who claims to be a former inhabitant. She

c

shows him her poems and performs a dance for him before disappearing. And in 'A Dream of Ch'in' (c. 827; *T'ang-jen hsiao-shuo*, pp.162–3), the author staying at a hostel outside Ch'ang-an built over the tomb of Duke Mu of Ch'in, enters the Duke's service in his dream and marries the Duke's daughter, Lung-yü, celebrated for her playing of the pipes.

Though fantasy is the keynote to the T'ang supernatural tale, its writers often give the impression that they are more concerned with veracity. Chronology is careful and exact, sources are authenticated, subsequent happenings briefly recounted for the sake of completeness, and a final comment added, in which the narrator pronounces judgement as in treating real persons and events. This is because the writers were, consciously or unconsciously, modelling themselves on the historical biography, as created in the Han by Ssu-ma Ch'ien (b. B.C. 145) in his 'Records of a Historian' with its scores of lively character portrayals in a historical context. The form ensures an orderly sequence of events and offers scope for characterization, as, for example, in 'Miss Jen', but the biographical framework is inimical to sustained illusion and obtrudes upon narrative unity. In time, fantasy began to assert itself, and by the ninth century some writers had abandoned the pretence of writing history. But the development was certainly not general, nor continuous, and many T'ang and later writers of tales adhered rigidly to the biographical style with no concession to the demands of narrative art.

3. SUNG

In the Sung, while supernatural tales continued to be written, they were seldom the colourful and robust accounts with a keen sense of wonder as in the hands of the T'ang writers. And indeed the prevailing rational outlook and carefully inculcated philosophical temper were inimical to further development of the *Ch'uan-ch'i* tale. In the Sung tales, response to the marvellous is already a little stereotyped; fantasy is confined by a body of traditional lore, with invention limited to the incidental and peripheral; and the prose style lacks the liveliness and zest of the writers of the T'ang, and their elegance as well. The tales, which often comprise episodes loosely fitted together, usually rely for their interest on history or antiquarianism, on ghost lore or doctrine, on poems or epistles from the pen of hero or heroine, with elements taken from earlier tales no longer a cause of surprise and frequently distracting to the progress of the story. The tales of the Sung tend, then, to be records of unusual happenings in the manner of the early supernatural tale, or imitations of T'ang, and still earlier, tales, or vehicles of moral lessons, and are thus somewhat artificial and wanting in spontaneity.

The most representative collection of Sung tales, including supernatural tales, is *Ch'ing-so kao-i* (Ku-tien ed. 1958) edited by Liu Fu of the eleventh century. It contains tales by various Sung writers as well as tales adapted from earlier sources; for these adaptations and for some of the unattributed tales, Liu himself was probably in part or wholly responsible. There are tales about foxes, about dragons, about the common run of ghosts, and ghosts with historical associations. While they do not particularly excel as tales about the supernatural, they are enlivened by revelations about the human desires and preoccupations that underlie and colour supernatural experience.

In 'Hsiao-lien' (*Ch'ing-so kao-i*, hou-chi, c. 3, pp.116–8), a fox concubine in the capital Pien (i.e. Kaifeng in Honan Province) who has to make her obeisances to the local deities on the last day of the lunar month, confesses to her husband official that, because she had been a jealous and spiteful woman in her last reincarnation, she has been born as a fox and must soon die, hunted down by hounds; she then vanishes. At the appointed time, he identifies her carcass among the dead foxes carried by some hunters and accords it a proper burial, an ending recalling 'Miss Jen' (see *infra*, pp. 45–56). In 'Visiting the West Pond in Spring' (*Ch'ing-so kao-i*, pieh-chi, c. 1, pp. 185–92), which incorporates somewhat clumsily details from various earlier tales, a jealous and vindictive fox in the capital (Kaifeng) is a model wife to her human husband while he remains devoted to her but, when he abandons her, ruins his life.

In 'The Strange Fish' (*Ch'ing-so kao-i*, hou-chi, pp. 120–1), a female dragon caught in a fisherman's net with a human face and the body of a tortoise in Canton rewards the benefactor who sets her free by asking someone at the market to sell him a large pearl at a tenth of its value. In 'The Red Snake' (*Ch'ing-suo kao-i*, hou-chi, pp. 172–4), Li Yüan rescues a tiny red snake from some herd boys, bathes its wounds and lets it loose among the thick grass. Returning to the same spot in Wukiang (in Kiangsu Province) a year later, he is accosted by a handsome youth, who invites Li to his home, a palace under a mountain beside the great lake, Tai-hu. There Li receives the thanks of the Dragon King for saving the life of the youth, who is the King's son; and in reward the King marries his daughter to Li, who takes his bride home. Later she helps him to pass his examinations through foreknowledge of all the questions, remaining with him for six years. (A version of this story in colloquial speech is to be found in the Ming *hua-pen* collection of c. 1620, *Ku-chin hsiao-shuo*, c. 34; Jen-min ed. 1958, pp. 503–11.)

In 'A Dream about a Dragon' (*Ch'ing-so kao-i*, hou-chi, c. 9, pp. 169–70), at the request of the dragon in the lake by his home, who appears in a dream as an old man dressed in white, Ts'ao Chün, a wealthy and prominent resident of Chenhsien (in Hunan Province) with distinguished ancestors long serving in distant parts, helps to defeat an invading dragon. As the dragons fight in the shape of two bulls, Ts'ao shoots an arrow from his bow into the shoulder of the invader. When, in a second dream, the resident dragon asks him to name his reward, Ts'ao expresses the desire that his descendants always enjoy official rank without ever having to leave the locality, in other words, that they occupy, generation after generation, the ceremonial office of sergeant-at-arms of the district. Though taken aback by the modesty of the request, the dragon concedes that Ts'ao is a wise man and grants his wish.

'The Mists on the Lake' (*Ch'ing-so kao-i*, Ch'ien-chi, c. 5, pp. 45 – 6) is about the ghost of a faithful woman. The hero, a student in the capital (Kaifeng), is reduced to such straits that his wife's father forces her to leave him and return to her own home, where she pines away and dies; following her dying behest, the hero exhumes her remains in the night and carries them back to his ancestral home in Kaoan (in Kiangsi Province.) But compelled by poverty to leave home again, he is followed in all his wanderings, though unknown to him, by his wife's ghost. In the end he becomes a fisherman in Yoyang (in Hunan Province) and her ghost appears to him in the mists on Tungting Lake, coming closer day after day until at last, his allotted span having been reached, she leads him into the water.

'I-niang' by Hung Mai (1123 – 1202) in his collection *I-chien chih* (Commercial Press ed. 1941, IV, c.9, pp. 65 – 6), though later in date than the tales in *Ch'ing-so kao-i*, is one of the more attractive tales in the early manner, omitting, as it does, the poems and the text of the invocation which are part of the story. In the troubled years of the Chin Tartar invasion of North China, a plaintive poem inscribed on the wall of an eating-house in a city in the north leads Yang Ts'ung-shan to follow the writer, Yang's cousin's wife, I-niang, and her companions to a large mansion. Standing alone outside it, sumptuously dressed with a silk scarf tied round her neck, I-niang tells him how she and her husband had been beset by the invaders; to save her honour, she had tried to behead herself, but had been rescued by the Tartar Chief's Consort, under whose protection she now is. She then asks Yang to return with news of her husband. Repairing to the same eating-house some days later, Yang finds another poem and identifies the writer as his cousin Han, I-niang's husband. Han, who had earlier succeeded in fleeing to the south, had now been sent by the Sung court on a peace mission to the Tartar Chief. Yang seeks out Han, who expresses disbelief about I-niang being still alive, having seen her die under her own sword. They go to the large mansion, behind which the graves of the Tartar Chief's Consort and I-niang are pointed out to them beside a hall enshrining the portraits of the dead ladies. When Han composes an invocation to I-niang and offers to rebury her in the south, her ghost comes forward, declaring that she does indeed wish to be buried near Han, but that he must then tend her grave with care and show his devotion by not marrying again. Han thereupon secretly disinters her bones and has them reburied in Chien-k'ang (i.e. Nanking). But when, a few years later, he remarries, I-niang appears to him in a dream, full of reproach, and Han dies of remorse.

In tales about the ghosts of historical figures, the ghost story is combined with an incursion into popular history. In Ch'in Ch'un's 'The Hot Springs' (*Ch'ing-so kao-i*, Ch'ien-chi, c. 6, pp. 58–61), the Sung official, Chang Yü, who is much preoccupied with the events of the reign of the Brilliant Emperor of the T'ang, while on a repeated visit to Li-shan to the east of the T'ang capital Ch'ang-an, with its palace and baths of the Emperor, composes some poems lamenting the glorious past. Some days later, he is summoned in his sleep before the Brilliant Emperor's Precious Consort, now a goddess, who commends his poems and presently invites him to join her, though stationed a few paces apart, in bathing in the hot springs, thereby re-enacting for him the celebrated scene of herself emerging from the bath in Ch'en Hung's tale (see *supra*, p. 24) and Po Chü-i's poem. The Precious Consort then questions Chang about women's fashions in the present and has some of her own clothes and jewellery brought forward for his inspection. Chang mildly reproves her for her intrigue with the ugly and treacherous An Lu-shan, but is mollified to learn, in response to his inquiry, that the Brilliant Emperor is now also a god. They retire for the night, the Precious Consort to her own bed and Chang to a bed placed beside it. From her bed he is magically debarred, though lying on his, he may converse with her. At dawn, she dismisses him with a small scented box tied to his wrist, and promises a further meeting twenty years hence.

In 'Fan Min' (*Ch'ing-so kao-i*, hou-chi, c. 6, pp. 146–50), the scholar Fan Min, benighted on his way to Yuncheng (in Shantung Province), enjoys the hospitality of the ghost of a palace lady, a musician much favoured by the music-loving Emperor Chuang-tsung of the Posterior T'ang. She plays on the pipes for him, and tells about the downfall and death of the Emperor and her own sad end as the concubine of a general. After many days, their intimacy is interrupted by the return of the ghost general, whose noisy quarrels with his ghost concubine and ghost friends, visible and invisible, eventually shatter the ghost dwelling. Fan finds himself among tombs, his bag empty, while a small boy approaches him with a message from the general: 'Even in the world of the living, whores must be paid for. For a fortnight's custom, our charges have really been very moderate'. He then discovers at a wine shop a dozen *li* ahead that someone has been exchanging the clothes in his bag for wine in the name of the graduate Fan.

In 'Courtier to the King of Ch'u' (*Ch'ing-so kao-i*, Pieh-chi, c. 7, pp. 225–8), the hero, who has fled from his home in Szechwan to the coast, is invited to the palace of Hsiang Yü, King of Ch'u, in the underworld and asked to compose an epistle exonerating a breach of etiquette on the part of the King. At the banquet that follows, the hero flirts with one of the royal concubines but, by appealing to historical precedent, convinces the enraged King that misbehaviour arising from momentary infatuation must be overlooked at a feast. At the command of the King, the hero discusses the tactical errors in his host's celebrated campaigns against the founding Emperor of the Han and, before being sent back, agrees to accept service under the King at the end of his earthly days.

This tale, in which a mortal is invited to be the amanuensis of a slow-witted deity, anticipates similar tales in the Ming collections, *Chien-teng hsin-hua* and *Chien-teng yü-hua*. As in those collections also, poems are sometimes quoted extensively in Sung tales seemingly for display. Poems do form part of the story in 'Love by the Long Bridge' (*Ch'ing-so kao-i*, ch'ien-chi, c. 5, pp. 49–51), in which the hero, attracted by the scenery of Wukiang (in Kiangsu Province), lingers in the vicinity and woos a girl he meets on the river by addressing verses to her fisherman father. The father and the daughter turn out to be immortals; they accept his suit and he leaves with them, to reappear years later as an immortal.

And in 'Ch'eng Yüeh' (*Ch'ing-so kao-i*, hou-chi, c. 3, pp. 123–5), a gaol-warder of Chenhsien (in Hunan Province), while on a boat journey to the capital (Kaifeng), is brought to the underworld to answer an accusation, but proves his innocence and makes a tour of hell before returning to his body.

More distinctively supernatural, though, as would be obvious from even this brief survey, not typical of the Sung supernatural tale, is the tale of 'Wang Hsieh' (see *infra*, pp. 103–9), which possesses in its simplicity a certain charm, unmarred by the clumsy artifice of the hero's name and the anachronistic quotation at the end. It is the only Sung tale among the translations in this volume.

4. Ming

In the Ming, the supernatural tale is revived by Ch'ü Yu (1341–1427), a native of Hangchow (in Chekiang Province), in the twenty tales,[1] all by himself, in his collection *Chien-teng hsin-hua* ('New Tales recounted by Lamplight', Preface 1378, ed. Chou I, Ku-tien 1957), seventeen of which deal with supernatural subjects. Though much indebted to T'ang and Sung models, Ch'ü's tales are artfully contrived and possess some degree of unity, not always to be found in earlier tales, even T'ang tales. In the tales in *Chien-teng hsin-hua*, the conduct of the story, though unexciting, is smooth and engaging; invention is limited, the characters and situations being often stereotyped; wonder and horror are couched in clichés, and seldom evoke a spontaneous response. Nevertheless Ch'ü's facility in narrative and description, and in the poems and prose compositions that ornament many of his tales, and his even tone and urbane manner charmed and impressed the cultivated reader of his day and stamp on his tales the mark of individual authorship.

A professed admirer of Ch'ü, Li Chen (1376 – 1452), whose home district was Lu-ling (i.e. Kian in Kiangsi Province) but who had occupied official positions in the capital Peking and in Kwangsi and Honan provinces, imitated *Chien-teng hsin-hua*, naming his own collection of tales *Chien-teng yü-hua* ('More Tales recounted by Lamplight', Preface 1420, included with the Ku-tien edition of *Chien-teng hsin-hua*), consisting also of twenty tales (with the addition of a long poem and a much longer tale written before he had ever come across Ch'ü's work), fourteen of them concerned with the supernatural. In theme and style, Li adheres fairly closely to his model, though in inventive skill he shows himself to advantage; his eagerness for display leads to a disproportionate representation of incidental prose and verse compositions extraneous to the story; he is also somewhat long-winded, so that Ch'ü's brevity and compactness frequently give way in Li's tales to elaboration and digression. In this, Li seems to have conceded to popular taste for the kind of story being told by the colloquial story-tellers of the time and surviving now in *hua-pen* collections of the sixteenth and seventeenth centuries.² In short, Li is a more vulgar version of Ch'ü, though Li's appeal is also to the cultivated reader, who is interested in good narrative, poetry, history, music and painting.

The subjects dealt with in the tales in *Chien'teng hsin-hua* and *Chien-teng yü-hua* include apes, dragons, foxes, immortals, visits to hell, ghosts, and goblins; and in the summaries that follow, Ch'ü's and Li's tales are lumped together. Since both collections are reprinted in a volume simply entitled *Chien-teng hsin-hua*, to avoid confusion, each tale cited is followed by the name of the author (Ch'ü or Li), the *chüan* of the collection in which it is found, and the page references in the Ku-tien edition of *Chien-teng hsin-hua*.

In 'Shen-yang Cave' (Ch'ü, c. 3, pp. 69–71), which is derived from the T'ang tale 'The White Ape' (see *supra*, p. 16), the hero adventures into the cave outside Kweilin (in Kwangsi Province) of an Ape spirit that has abducted three beautiful girls, and kills the ape and its followers; and the grateful families of the girls marry all of them to him with large dowries. And in 'The Ape who listened' (Li, c. 1, pp. 139–44), which combines the ape story with Buddhist doctrine, an ape who listens day after day to a famous monk chanting his sutras in front of his temple in Kishui (in Kiangsi Province) adopts human guise and becomes a disciple to the monk, though betraying, in the role of novice, apish manners and a monkeyish restlessness.

In 'Celebrations in the Under-water Palace' (Ch'ü, c. 1, pp. 11–14), a scholar of Chaochow (in Kwangtung Province) is asked by the Dragon King of the South China Sea to compose an inscription commemorating a hall to be erected in the King's under-water palace, and stays to compose a song at the inauguration ceremony, attended by three other Dragon Kings. The inscription, in a style of mock solemnity, is in part reminiscent of the River Lord's decree in the T'ang tale 'The Carp' (*infra*, pp. 71–5) and a red carp does indeed invite itself to the ceremony but is angrily packed off.

And in 'The Dragon King's Banquet' (Ch'ü, c. 4, pp. 86–90), dragon lore is combined with history. The sight of a white dragon appearing like a perpendicular jade pillar among the clouds at Wukiang (in Kiangsu Province), its scales shining in the sun like hundreds of mirrors, inspires the hero to write a poem in praise of the Dragon King. In consequence, he is invited to the Dragon King's banquet, attended by the spirits of several worthies of the Wu region, one of whom, Wu Tzu-hsü, Minister of Wu in the Chou dynasty, challenges the claims of another, Fan Li, Minister of Yüeh, to be the pre-eminent exemplar of virtue in the region.

In 'The Alluring Fox' (Li, c. 3, pp. 238–40), the concubine of an Assistant Prefectural Magistrate in Yaohsien (in Shensi Province) who calls herself Hu Mei-niang ('The Alluring Fox') and is originally from Sincheng (in Honan Province), is impeccable in her behaviour and wise in her counsel to her husband, who, however, falls unaccountably ill. Under exorcism by a Taoist priest, the concubine is struck by a thunderbolt and discovered to be a dead fox with a human skull sitting on its head.

About immortals, there is 'A Boat Trip on Chien Lake by night' (Ch'ü, c. 4, pp. 102–5), in which the hero, adrift on his boat by night among the Kuei-chi (i.e. Huichi) Mountains (in Chekiang Province), is borne by the wind and waves to the Milky Way. There he meets the goddess, the Weaving Maid, who enjoins him to refute all the slanderous love stories concerning herself and the Herd Boy spread by poets and chroniclers. And in 'An Encounter with Immortals' (Li, c. 3, pp. 230–4) the ethereal background anticipates similar settings in the Ch'ing collection of tales, *Liao-chai chih-i*. The hero Tu Chuan-ch'eng ties his boat under a cliff in the Wuyi Mountains (in Fukien Province) and, walking through a stone gate, comes to a Taoist temple named 'Azure's Hermitage' with a high wall and ornate buildings, before which cranes stalk about and monkeys frisk among the willows and orchids. He is led into the presence of Master

Azure, namely Tu Pen of the Yüan dynasty, who announces
that he is an ancestor of the hero's and houses the hero in a
room with a bamboo couch and a stone pillow, lit by moon-
light and penetrated by the wind and snowflakes. A day later,
seven other immortals, among them celebrated Yüan
painters and poets, call on Master Azure, who introduces the
hero as his descendant, summoned to rescue from the torrents
a sealed stone box containing the manuscript of Master
Azure's study of The Annals of Spring and Autumn and its
Commentaries in 48 *chüan*, hidden in a cliff and only to be
revealed to a kindred spirit. The immortals paint pictures
or inscribe prose and verse compositions on a handscroll for
the hero, who returns with this treasure to his boat, later
locating the stone box and depositing it in another part of
the cliff.

In 'A Dream of Hell' (Ch'ü, c. 2, pp. 36–8), a sceptical
scholar is arraigned before the nether courts for his
irreverence in doubting the justice of the infernal world, but
is acquitted and shown round the various torture chambers
before he is sent home. Similarly in 'A Tour of the Underworld' (Li, c.1, pp.162–7), the hero, a staunch Confucian
given to refuting Buddhist and Taoist beliefs, is brought
before an infernal court for his impiety, after which,
thoroughly repentant, he is taken on a tour of hell, for one of
whose exits, 'The Gate of Fleeting Existence', he composes
an inscription before returning to his inert body.

Lovers predominate in tales about ghosts. The Phoenix-
shaped Hairpin' (Ch'ü, c.1, pp. 26–9) is derived from the
T'ang tale 'Twixt Soul and Body' (*infra*, pp. 59–61) with
the addition of a second heroine to enable the dead to be
with the living. The heroine Hsing-niang, daughter of a
Yangchow (in Kiangsu Province) family, dies after pining
for her long absent affianced and is buried with the gold
phoenix-shaped hairpin that was his betrothal gift. The
fiancé Ts'ui returns, and is visited at night by a girl claiming
to be the heroine's younger sister, Ch'ing-niang. After a

month, they elope, finding shelter in Tanyang (in Kiangsu
Province) in the home of a farmer, a former servant. A year
or so later, the wife expressing a longing for home, they
return to Yangchow, and leaving her in the boat, Ts'ui calls
on her father to apologize for his offence in running away
with Ch'ing-niang and to beg for forgiveness. His story is
greeted with incomprehension even when he presents the
phoenix-shaped hairpin, which his wife has asked him to
produce as a token; and a servant dispatched to the boat
finds no-one on it. But Ch'ing-niang, who has lain ill in the
house for a year, now rises from her bed and speaks in the
voice of her dead sister, Hsing-niang: she, Hsing-niang,
had, in the guise of Ch'ing-niang, followed her betrothed to
Tanyang, but is about to return to the world of the shades,
her place to be taken, her parents being willing, by her sister,
Ch'ing-niang, whose union with Ts'ui has her blessing.
Then fondly bidding Ts'ui farewell and asking him to cherish
her, she falls to the ground dead, but presently revives and
is well again, and the parents marry Ch'ing-niang to
Ts'ui.

In 'Ts'ui-ts'ui' (Ch'ü, c. 4, pp. 78–83), a husband, whose
wife, Ts'ui-ts'ui, was taken captive in the wars at Hwaian
(in Kiangsu Province), traces her, after a long and circuitous
search, to the house of a General Li in Huchow (in Chekiang
Province), whose favourite concubine she now is, and
claiming to be her brother, is taken into service by the
general. But although he and Ts'ui-ts'ui manage once to
exchange a poem, they realize that they can only be reunited
in death and, dying one after the other, are buried side by
side. A former servant of her family happening years later to
be in the vicinity, the ghost couple invite him to their house,
offer him entertainment and entrust him with an epistle to
her parents describing their happiness in being reunited.
And the ghosts of the pair appear to her father when, led
thither by his daughter's epistle, he finds only their tombs.
The poems and epistle are retained in Ling Meng-ch'u's

version of this story in colloquial speech in *Erh-k'o P'ai-an ching-ch'i* (1632), c.6, (Ku-tien ed. 1957, pp.133–47).

Other tales tell about ghosts of earlier periods in history. In 'The Maid in Green' (Ch'ü, c.4, pp.107–10), the hero is visited in his lodgings beside the house of the Sung Prime Minister Chia Ssu-tao on Ko Hill in Hangchow by the ghost of his beloved in a previous reincarnation, in which he had been the tea attendant and she the chess maid in the Prime Minister's establishment. When their innocent love for each other had been discovered, they had both been put to death by the Prime Minister, whose cruel deeds the ghost recounts. After three years, the ghost of the beloved expires, leaving an empty coffin.

In 'A Nocturnal Adventure outside Ch'ang-an' (Li, c.1, pp.133–6), a ghost couple of the T'ang, a cake-seller and his wife, celebrated for their fidelity in a T'ang collection of anecdotes, offer the hero, who is on his way back from Hingping to Sian (in Shensi Province), hospitality for the night and beg him to publish their true story. Because of her beauty, the wife had been abducted by their neighbour, Prince Ning, who giving way to her passive resistance, had, after a month, restored her unharmed to her husband; she had not been a member of the Prince's household for a whole year before being released out of compassion by the Prince, as in existing accounts. The couple, who refuse to divulge their names, each tell their story in a poem, and the hero arranges for the poems to be carved on stone for posterity.

In 'Hsüeh T'ao' (Li, c.2, pp.179–86), the talented T'ien Chu encounters, in a peach grove outside Chengtu (in Szechwan Province), the ghost of the T'eng courtesan, Hsüeh T'ao, and vies with her in verse composition night after night, in 'Chü-ching Garden' (Ch'ü, c.2, pp.46–9), the hero visits the Sung Imperial Chü-ching Garden by the West Lake in Hangchow on a summer's night and comes upon the ghost of a Sung palace lady. They continue to meet in a pavilion, and she follows him to his home in Wenchow (in

Chekiang Province) but, after three years, returns with him to Hangchow, where she disappears. In 'Playing on the Guitar under the Moon' (Li, c.1, pp.147–56), the ghost of the maidservant of a militantly chaste lady of the Sung appears to the hero while he is playing on his guitar at night in Yungsin (in Kiangsi Province), and requests him to instal a tablet to her in the shrine dedicated to the memory of her mistress, later rewarding him by giving him the score of the long-lost suite for guitar, 'Kuang-ling san' (cf. the early tale 'Chi K'ang', *supra*, p.9).

In some of the tales, clay figures and other inanimate objects become spirits. In 'The Peony Lantern' (Ch'ü, c.2, pp.52–5), a widower is attracted by the 'double peony' lantern carried by a maidservant lighting the way for a young lady on the evening of the Festival of Lanterns in Ningpo (in Chekiang Province), and invites them to his home. The lady turns out to be the ghost of a girl whose coffin has lain unburied for years in a pavilion in the middle of a lake, and her maid, a funerary figure under a 'double peony' lantern in front of the coffin. Eventually the lady lures the widower into her coffin and the lid closes upon them both, after which three ghosts, instead of two, are to be seen wandering in the night with a peony lantern. An exorcism follows : chained and shackled by infernal agents, all three write their confessions in elegant phrases. In 'The Clay Goddesses' (Li, c.4, pp.254–9), four beautiful girls, who first appear to the hero in the garden of his uncle's mansion and subsequently visit him in his room, are discovered to be four clay figures in a shrine dedicated to a love goddess in a temple overlooking the river in Meishan (in Szechwan Province), their gifts to him of gold and silver ornaments later turning into clay. When alarmed relatives wreck the clay figures and sink them in the river, the spell is broken.

'Goblins in a Wuping Monastery' (Li, c.3, pp.217–22), an imitation of the T'ang tales 'Goblins in the Night at a Tung-yang Temple' and 'Yüan Wu-yu' (see *supra*, pp.19–20), tells of the adventures by night of the hero in an abandoned monastery in Wuping (in Fukien Province), where he had been accustomed to stay in former years. In the dark, a clay image, a chipped inkstone, a worn writing brush, a pot without a handle, a stew-pan covered with dust, a threadbare quilt, a skull-shaped wooden block for the chanting of sutras, a coffin lid and a torn silk fan engage in Buddhist argument and declaim verses revealing their identity.

Even more than in the Sung, the supernatural tale in the Ming is about people in celestial or phantom dress and placed in an exotic setting. In other words, the Ming supernatural tale is a 'costume' supernatural tale dealing with mundane passions and concerns under a supernatural guise without much probing into the nature of supernatural experience. In it, ghostly horror and heavenly glory are alike artificial, and the paraphernalia of infernal machinery and Buddhist and Taoist eschatology loom large and threaten to engulf the story. But the tales of Ch'ü and Li are well told and occasionally felicitious in language; and they contain much pathos, especially the fortunes of lovers, living and spectral, movingly recounted. The tales generally, and in particular the descriptive passages in them, frequently convey colour and light effects and a pictorial neatness and elegance that suggest the hand of some Ming painter. Nevertheless the Ming supernatural tale is but a pale reflection of the supernatural world. It is only in the Ch'ing that P'u Sung-ling (1640–1715) in his *Liao-chai chih-i* (see *infra*, pp.113–69) reactivates the supernatural imagination and reasserts the primacy of supernatural experience, thereby raising the supernatural tale to new heights.

1. There is an additional tale, largely factual, about two lovers in an Appendix based on the life of one of the author's friends.
2. See General Introduction to Volume I of this series, *Popular Fiction and Drama*, pp. 6–13, 'Story-telling'.

'Miss Jen'

At the age of fifty, a fox can change into a woman. At the age of a hundred, it can change into a beautiful girl or a wizard or a man who seduces women; it can know about happenings a thousand *li* distant; it can bewitch people, leading them astray and causing them to lose their wits. At the age of a thousand, it can communicate with heaven and become a celestial fox.

This short discourse, which heads the section 'The Fox' (c. 447 – c. 455) in the compilation *T'ai-p'ing kuang-chi* (978), c. 447, p. 3652, underlies all Chinese fox lore. It was taken from *Hsüan-chung chi* by the mythologist Kuo P'u (276–324). The 'New Ballads' of the T'ang poet Po Chü-i contains one entitled 'The Fox in an Ancient Tomb', the first half of which reads:

A fox inhabiting an ancient tomb,
Old and skilled at sorcery,
Transforms itself into a woman of handsome features,
Head covered with black hair, face painted with powder,
And the ungainly tail turned into a long red robe.
Slowly it paces the road near some deserted village,
Where the sun is setting and the place secluded,
Singing or dancing or weeping bitterly,
With eyebrows knit and countenance abject,
Then suddenly smiles with infinite bewitchment,

D

Misleading nine onlookers out of ten.
If feigned beauty so beguiles,
How much more so real beauty?
> (*Po Hsiang-shan chi*, c. 4, Wen-hsüeh ku-chi ed., II,
> p. 54)

In the tale 'The Monk Yen-t'ung' in *T'ai-p'ing kuang-chi*, c. 451, a fox tries out four or five human skulls before finding one that would sit firmly on its head, and then, covering itself with some leaves and straw, changes into a woman (p. 3691; see also 'Liu Yüan-ting', c. 454, p. 3709). A fox transforms itself into a monk leading a procession of women into a tomb in 'Yeh Fa-shan' (c. 448, pp. 3665–6), and into a Taoist reading a manuscript also in a tomb in 'Li Tzu-liang' (c. 453, pp. 3700–1). The fox may assume the shape of a Buddha or Bodhisatva, as in 'The Monk Fu-li' (c. 447, pp. 3658–9), 'Adjutant T'ang' (c. 450, pp. 3677–8), 'Inhabitant of Tai-chou' (c. 450, p. 3683) and 'Chang-sun Chia' (c. 451, pp. 3685–6); or it may appear disguised as a departed parent, as in 'Yen Chien' (c. 450, pp. 3680–1; see also 'Hsin T'i-fou', c. 450, p. 3682).

The fox may transform itself into a young man and lover, as in 'Hsü An' (c. 450, pp. 3679–80) and 'Li Yüan-kung' (c. 449, pp. 3671–2). A spell is usually cast on the lady love, as in 'Chang-sun Wu-chi' (c. 447, p. 3657), though the fox is often invisible, as in 'Chang Li-pen' (c. 454, pp. 3709–10) and 'Adjutant Wei' (c. 450, pp. 3681–2), or only appears (as a young man) after some time, as in 'Li Yüan-kung'. Or the fox appears as a woman, as in 'Shang-kuan I' (c. 447, p. 3659) and 'Wang Pao' (c. 450, p. 3677).

Frequently the fox insists on contracting a marriage alliance, as in 'Ho-lan Chin-ming' (c. 451, p. 3684) and 'Wang Hsüan' (c. 451, p. 3689), in which the fox-bride is careful to adhere to all the niceties of conventional etiquette. In 'Chi Chen' (c. 454), the hero Chi Chen, who is intoxicated, falls off his horse at night outside Shan-hsien (i.e. Sanmenhsia in Honan Province) and loses sight of his servants while on a journey to the capital. He comes upon a country mansion and is invited into a guest chamber which is furnished with elegance and taste. He is also charmed with his host, a man of fifty or so, with whom, when pressed, he stays for a further night. Then, in the capital, Chi is visited by a stranger, who brings forward a proposal from his late host that Chi should marry his daughter. After some time, Chi calls on his former host again and marries the daughter, who is beautiful and clever and gentle. Chi returns home with his wife, who also accompanies him to his official post. She gives birth to seven sons and two daughters, and after twenty years looks as young and beautiful as ever. Suddenly she falls incurably ill. On the point of death, she confesses to him that she is a fox and makes him promise to give her a human burial. She then covers her head with the quilt and expires. When he removes the quilt, he finds a dead fox on the bed. Subsequently the children all die, but their corpses are human (pp. 3707−9).

But, for all its powers of transformation, the fox is sometimes unable to dispose of its tail, which obtrudes at inconvenient moments. In the early tale[1] 'Sun Yen' (c. 447, p. 3655), a husband discovers after three years of marriage that his wife has a fox-tail three feet in length. In 'Inhabitant of Ch'i-hsien' (c. 450, p. 3683), a woman clad in white, who begs for a lift in a cart, is discovered to have a fox-tail. When the owner of the cart cuts off the tail, the woman turns into a tail-less white fox. Fear of dogs would seem to be common to most foxes, the sight of dogs being sufficient to annihilate their faculty of metamorphosis. In 'Son of the Wei family' (c. 454, p. 3712), a woman changes into a fox on the appearance of dogs. In 'Villager of Ts'ang-chu' (c. 455, pp. 3718−9), a woman killed by a dog is found to be a dead fox. In 'Adjutant Li' (c. 448), a studious old man whom the hero meets at the inn in Sincheng (in Honan Province) advises the hero, Adjutant Li, to seek a wife among the daughters of the Hsiao family, and offers to act as intermediary.

Li calls on the father of the family and is impressed by his appearance and manner. The bride, too, is exceedingly beautiful. Li brings her and her numerous maids to his post. After two years, a colleague of Li's about to go on a hunt passes Li's door with his hounds. The maids are terrified by the dogs and retreat into the house. His suspicions aroused, the colleague pushes open the window and lets the dogs loose in the house, whereupon all the fox-maidservants are killed. Li's wife, too, is killed, but her corpse remains human, though with a fox-tail (pp. 3666–8).

'Miss Jen' is the first of seven tales from the T'ang included in this volume. Its author was Shen Chi-chi, a man from Soochow (in Kiangsu Province) who was active in the second half of the eighth century. Shen was a historian and, for some time, a compiler in the Bureau of History occupying the rank at court of Reminder. After his banishment to Ch'u-chou (i.e. Lishui in Chekiang Province), mentioned in our tale without specifying the exact place of exile, he was recalled and ended as a Second Class Secretary in the Board of Rites. His biography may be found in *Chiu T'ang shu*, c.149, punctuated ed., pp. 4034–7, and *Hsin T'ang shu*, c.132, punctuated ed., pp. 4538–40.

Shen also wrote 'The Pillow', a tale about the vanity of human life (*T'ang-jen hsiao-shuo*, pp. 37–9). 'Miss Jen' is in *T'ang-jen hsiao-shuo*, pp. 43–8, and *T'ai-p'ing kuang-chi*, c. 452, pp. 3692–7.

1. Among the tales from *T'ai-p'ing kuang-chi* cited in this and the following Introductions, those written before the T'ang are designated 'early', while the others would be from the T'ang or the tenth century; tales which could be earlier than the T'ang are described as 'probably early'.

Miss Jen

Miss Jen was a fox spirit. There was the Prefect Wei Yin, who was, on his mother's side, grandson of the Prince of Hsin-an, ranking ninth among his cousins, and who, in his youth, was wild and fond of drinking. One of Yin's female cousins married Cheng Sixth, whose personal name I have forgotten; though accomplished in the military arts and fond of wine and women, Cheng was so poor that he had no home of his own and lived with his wife's relations. Yin and Cheng were the best of friends and quite inseparable.

In the sixth month of the ninth year (750) of the T'ien-pao reign, Yin and Cheng were in a street in the capital Ch'ang-an (i.e. Sian in Shensi Province), going together to a feast in Hsin-ch'ang Ward. On reaching the southern end of Hsüan-p'ing Ward, Cheng excused himself, saying that he would join Yin later, and while Yin turned eastwards on his white horse, Cheng went south on his donkey, entering the north gate of Sheng-p'ing Ward. Three women happening to be walking in the street, one of whom, dressed in white, was unusually beautiful, Cheng was much attracted and contrived now to precede and now to follow them, timidity only restraining him from addressing them. But the woman in white would often look at him, as if susceptible to his attentions, whereupon Cheng said in jest, 'So fine a lady should not be pacing the streets of Ch'ang-an'. The woman

said laughing, 'If some people who are mounted would not
lend us their beast, what may we do?' Cheng then said, 'A
donkey is hardly fit to carry a lady, but have mine for the
present. I shall be content to follow on foot'. And Cheng and
the woman looked at each other and burst out laughing; her
companions presently joining in the exchanges, all were soon
on familiar terms. Cheng followed them eastwards to the
Pleasure Gardens, by which time it was dusk, and they
stopped outside a gate in a mud wall, behind which rose an
imposing residence. The woman in white said to Cheng,
'Pray stay a moment' and went in, and one of her companions,
a servant girl left behind by the gate, asked Cheng his name
and rank in the family. Cheng gave his reply and proceeded
to ask about her mistress, and the girl said, 'She is Miss Jen,
and twentieth among her cousins'. Soon afterwards, Cheng
was invited in. Having tied his donkey by the gate and placed
his hat on the saddle, he was greeted by a woman over
thirty, who turned out to be Miss Jen's sister. Candles were
lit and food spread out; the wine flowing freely, they were
joined by Miss Jen, who had changed her clothes, and all
three passed a merry evening, drinking to their hearts'
content. It being then late, Cheng retired with Miss Jen,
whose peerless beauty, aided by her melodious voice, pealing
laughter and graceful movements, made her seem divine, not
of this world.

Before dawn, Miss Jen said to Cheng, 'You must go! My
brother, who is in the employ of the Bureau of Entertain-
ments, is on duty in the Southern Hall in the Palace, and will
come out at dawn. Do not tarry!' Having made her promise
they would meet again, Cheng left. The gate of the Ward
being still locked, a Tartar pastry-seller in his shop by the
gate had just lit his lamp to start a fire in the stove, and
while waiting for the drum to sound, Cheng took shelter
under the pastry-seller's curtain and chatted to the man.
Pointing in the direction of the place where he had spent the
night, Cheng said, 'If you turn east from here, you will see a

gate; whose house does it open into?' The pastry-seller replied, 'It is all waste land behind a wall; there is no house'. Exclaiming, 'But I just passed a house! Why do you say there is none?' Cheng began to argue heatedly with the man, who suddenly nodded to himself and said, 'Oh, I know what it is! There is a fox here who lures men to her lair in the waste ground. I have seen it happen three times. I suppose you, too, have been enticed by her'. Ashamed, Cheng denied this, and when it was broad daylight, went back to the spot and found the gate and mud wall, through which he glimpsed only a neglected market garden overgrown with weeds.

When Cheng went home, he met Yin, who reproached him for not keeping his appointment the night before, but concealing his adventure, Cheng lied about where he had been. Nevertheless, he remembered and cherished Miss Jen's charms and longed to see her again. After over ten days, going into a clothes stall in the Western Market, he suddenly caught sight of her with the same servant girl. When he cried out aloud to her, she turned aside and mingled with the crowd to avoid him. But he pressed forward and continued to call to her, and she then stood with her back to him, covering her posterior with a fan,[1] saying, 'Now that you know what I am, why do you come near me?' Cheng said, 'Even if I do know, what difference does it make?' Miss Jen then said, 'I am quite ashamed of myself and cannot face you.' Cheng said, 'I have pined for you all these days; how can you now bear to cast me aside?' Miss Jen said, 'How dare I cast you aside? I was only afraid that you would regard me with loathing'. Thereupon Cheng swore his love for her, pleading with her in great earnest, and at last, Miss Jen turned round and removed her fan, showing herself to be as dazzlingly beautiful as she had been before. She then said, 'There are many women who are as pleasing in appearance as I. It just happens that you have not met them. Do not stare at me in wonder!' Cheng now asking for an assignation,

Miss Jen continued: 'My compeers are shunned by men for this reason only—they cause men to waste away. But I am harmless and quite different from them, and if you, sir, as you say, look upon me with favour, I shall be happy to serve you all my life'.

Cheng then promising to find a house for her, Miss Jen said, 'In a secluded lane to the east of this market, there is a house with a large tree jutting out from the roof, which you can rent. The gentleman on the white horse who on that occasion left you at the south gate of Hsüan-p'ing Ward and turned eastwards—is he not your wife's cousin? He has a lot of furniture which you can borrow'. At the time several of Yin's uncles had been posted to outer parts, their furniture being all stored in Yin's home. Following Miss Jen's instructions, Cheng found the house and rented it, and then went to Yin for the supply of domestic furnishings. When Yin asked what it was all about, Cheng said, 'I am setting up home with a charmer I met and need the furniture for her use'. Yin said laughing, 'A charmer? To judge by your own features, more likely a hag!' And Yin lent Cheng hangings and curtains, beds and mats.

Yin then sent one of his clever servants to follow Cheng to the house and spy on the lady. The servant returning in a great hurry, panting and streaming with sweat, Yin, who was waiting for him, asked, 'Is there a lady?' and added: 'Is she pretty?' The servant replied, 'It is quite extraordinary. There is no one so good-looking in all the world!' Yin, who had a large number of relatives and clansmen and who had seen something of the world and known many beautiful women, then asked whether a certain lady was more beautiful than Miss Jen, to which the servant replied, 'Not her equal!' And Yin mentioned four or five others, with the servant giving the same answer. At the time the sixth daughter of the Prince of Wu, to whom Yin was related, was regarded by all as the most beautiful among the cousins, for she was as exquisite as a goddess. So Yin finally asked, 'And how does the sixth daughter of the Prince of Wu compare with Miss Jen?' The servant again replying, 'Not her equal', Yin clapped his hands and cried in amazement, 'Is there really such a woman in this world?' And at once he had water fetched, washed his face and neck, daubed his lips, put on a turban, and made straight for Cheng's house.

Cheng happening to be out, Yin went inside and found a page boy sweeping the floor with a broom, and a servant girl standing at the door, but no one else. Yin inquired of the page, who said, smiling, 'There is no lady'. Yin then took a good look round the room and, seeing part of a red skirt protruding from under a door, went up close and found Miss Jen hiding behind it. And Yin dragged Miss Jen into the open and studied her face, and saw that she was even more beautiful than had been reported to him. Being now madly in love with Miss Jen, Yin folded her in his arms, intending to ravish her, but she would not yield. Then Yin tried to have his will by force, whereupon, desperate, she said, 'I surrender. Let go a moment!' But when he loosened his grip, she continued to repel him as before. After this had happened three or four times, Yin used all his strength to overcome Miss Jen, who was now pouring with sweat and utterly exhausted. Thinking it useless to oppose him, she no longer struggled, and her expression changed into one of mournfulness. Yin asked, 'But why are you so displeased?' Heaving a sigh, Miss Jen said, 'Poor Cheng Sixth!' Yin said, 'What do you mean?' Miss Jen replied, 'That a man six foot in height cannot even protect a woman—is that not cause for shame? Besides, you were always gay and gallant, and enjoyed the love of many beautiful women, my equal or superior. But Master Cheng is without means, and I am his sole delight. Will you not in your surfeit forgo what to another is his only comfort? I do pity the man for his destitute state, who, being without independency, could lay claim to nothing of his own. Why, the very clothes he wears belonged to you and the food he feeds on comes from you, so that he is chained to you like a slave. If he had been able to provide for his own needs, it would never have come to this!' Yin, who, being a perfect cavalier, was not devoid of notions of right conduct and obligation, heard her out and desisted. Straightening his garments as a sign of respect, he said, 'I have been at fault'. Soon afterwards Cheng came in, and Yin and Cheng looked at each other and smiled, and remained the best of friends. And from that time on, Yin supplied all that was needed—firewood, grain, lambs and pigs—in Miss Jen's home.

Miss Jen often entertained or went visiting. She would go about in a carriage or sedan-chair or ride or walk. Yin was constantly with her, and they were on the most intimate terms, yet stopped short of the least misconduct. And Yin loved and esteemed Miss Jen all the more, constantly remembering her and never grudging her any favours. Miss Jen, who knew that he loved her, said to him, 'Unworthy that I am, you have bestowed your love on me, and I am unable to requite it and satisfy you, especially since I cannot break my vows to Master Cheng. My people are from Ch'in (i.e. Shensi Province) and I was born in Ch'ang-an. We were musicians and entertainers, and among our relatives, many are concubines in great families. Thus we know all the back lanes of Ch'ang-an. If you fancy a lady difficult of access, I can obtain her for you, and in that way repay your goodness to me'. Yin said, 'How splendid!'. Yin had been attracted by a woman clothes-vendor at the market called Chang Fifteenth, whose complexion was alabaster white, and he now asked if Miss Jen knew her. Miss Jen said, 'She is related to a cousin of mine, and easy to come by'. And Miss Jen brought about a secret meeting between the woman and Yin ten days or so later, but after several months he tired of her.

Miss Jen then said to Yin, 'It is easy to succeed with people of the market, for which you hardly need my assistance. But if you aspire to someone kept in seclusion and above your reach, let me know and I will do my utmost for you'. Yin said, 'At the Festival of Cold Food the other day, I went with some companions to Thousand Blessings Temple, where General Tiao Mien had musicians in the great hall, among them a girl aged sixteen or so who played on the pipes. She had two knots of hair over her ears and was extremely good-looking. Do you know her?' Miss Jen said, 'Oh, that's "The Favourite", whose mother is a cousin of mine! I can secure her for you'. Then Yin bowed to request the favour, and Miss Jen consented. She then made several visits to the Tiao residence, and after a month, when Yin enquired how her plans were shaping, she merely asked for two rolls of silk as a bribe for someone, which Yin gladly handed over to her. Two days later, when she and Yin were having a meal, an old steward of General Tiao's came with a carriage to fetch Miss Jen, who, on hearing about the summons, said to Yin, smiling, 'You will soon accomplish your design'. For Miss Jen had put 'The Favourite' under a spell, causing an illness which medicine and the needle could not cure. When the girl's mother and the general, who were both very worried about her, thought of consulting a sorceress, Miss Jen secretly bribed the sorceress, asking her to propose that 'The Favourite' move to Miss Jen's house, carefully indicating the locality. And when the sorceress was then brought to the sick-bed, she said, 'The lady must not remain in this house. Let her be removed to a house in the south-east, whence she would derive the spirit of life'. Upon studying the sorceress' instructions, the general and the girl's mother concluded that 'The Favourite' should move to Miss Jen's, and the general made a request to this effect to Miss Jen, who feigned unwillingness to accept 'The Favourite' on the excuse that her house was too small, finally giving her consent only after repeated requests. 'The Favourite' was then sent in a carriage, along with her mother and her clothes and possessions, to Miss Jen's house, upon reaching which, her illness vanished. A few days later, Miss Jen sent for Yin and 'The Favourite' became his mistress. But after a month 'The Favourite' was with child, and her mother, in alarm, hurriedly took her back to General Tiao's, and the affair came to an end.

One day, Miss Jen said to Cheng, 'I want you to make some profit in a business venture. Can you lay hold of five or six thousand cash?' Cheng assented and borrowed six thousand cash. Miss Jen then said, 'Someone at the market is offering to sell a horse with a mark on its thigh. Buy it, and hold it until the price rises'. At the market, Chen indeed found a man leading a horse with a mark on its left thigh for sale, which Cheng bought and took home, only to be derided by his wife and her brothers, who exclaimed, 'But the jade is worn-out with use! Why did you buy it?' Before many days had elapsed, Miss Jen said to Cheng, 'You can sell the horse now. You should get thirty thousand cash'. And Cheng went to the market with the horse, but refused to sell it when someone offered him twenty thousand. And people all over the market were asking, 'Why should anybody want to buy a horse like that at such a price? And why should anybody refuse to sell it at that price?' Then Cheng got on his horse and returned home, followed by the man who kept on raising his offer until it reached twenty-five thousand. Cheng insisting on thirty thousand, again his wife and her brothers abused him, so that eventually he was compelled to sell it for something less than that amount. To discover why the purchaser had bought the horse, Cheng afterwards sought out the man, who turned out to be a groom of the Imperial stables in Chao-ying County (i.e. Lintung), where a horse with a mark on its thigh had died three years ago but had not been reported at the time, so that for three years he had been able to keep for himself the grain ration for the dead horse. Since to replace a horse of the Imperial stables would cost sixty thousand cash, a substitute at thirty thousand was still cheap.

And because her clothes were much worn, Miss Jen asked

Yin to get her new ones. When Yin offered to give her lengths of silk of the best design, she would not have them, saying that she preferred ready-made garments. Yin then asked Chang Eldest of the market to make the purchases on her behalf, arranging for Chang to see Miss Jen to find out what she wanted. But after meeting Miss Jen, Chang said to Yin in a state of agitation, 'Surely the lady is from another world, a royal mistress or concubine whom you have abducted! Take my advice and restore her at once, lest disaster befall you!' Such indeed was the bewitching beauty of Miss Jen! And Yin never understood why she insisted on having ready-made garments instead of making her own clothes.

After over a year, Cheng was appointed Deputy Military Officer of Huai-li Prefecture,[2] to be stationed for a brief period at Chin-ch'eng (i.e. Lanchow in Kansu Province). For Cheng had his wife, who lived with her relatives, and although he was free to spend his time in the day, at night he was obliged to return to her, so that he and Miss Jen never spent many nights together. Now that he was taking up his post, he asked Miss Jen to accompany him. But she was reluctant to join him, saying that there was not a great deal of fun in their being together for just ten days or a month, and that she would rather he provided her with food to enable her to wait patiently for his return. The more Cheng entreated her, the more she persisted in her refusal. Cheng then requested that Yin provide for Miss Jen's needs in his absence, and Yin joined in the conversation, asking why she would not go. After a long hesitation, Miss Jen said that a sorceress had warned her against journeying westwards in that year. But Cheng, whose only thought was that they should be together, laughed with Yin, saying, 'So clever and yet so deceived!' and again insisted that Miss Jen accompany him. She replied, 'If there be truth in the sorceress's warning, then I should die merely to comply with your whim!' The two men dismissing her fears and again imploring

her to travel with Cheng, Miss Jen could no longer refuse
and agreed to go.

Having lent Miss Jen his horse, Yin gave her and Cheng
a farewell feast at nearby Lin-kao, where they waved to one
another and parted. After spending two nights on the road,
Miss Jen and Cheng reached Ma-wei (west of Hingping),
Miss Jen on her horse in front, Cheng on his donkey behind
her, followed by her maid on another mount. At the time a
groom of the Western Gate had been training his hounds in
Lochwan[3] for the past ten days, and as Cheng and Miss Jen
rode on, the dogs rushed out of the long grass. At that
instant, Cheng saw Miss Jen suddenly fall off her horse,
turn into a fox and run towards the south. Shouting and
hooting at the dogs, Cheng chased after them, but could not
stop them from pursuing their prey; after only one *li*, they
caught up with it and killed it. With tears in his eyes, Cheng
took out some money to redeem the dead fox from the
huntsman; and he buried it, marking the spot with a wooden
stick planted in the earth. Then turning to look at the horse,
he found it grazing by the road, with Miss Jen's clothes on
the saddle and her socks and shoes on the stirrups, like the
exuviae left behind by the cicada. And her ornaments were
scattered over the road. There was nothing else to be seen,
and her maid, too, had vanished.

When, after over ten days, Cheng returned to Ch'ang-an,
he was greeted with delight by Yin, who at once asked, 'How
is dear little Jen?' Cheng replied, weeping, 'She is dead'.
Yin was moved to tears, and the two men clasped each other,
giving way to their grief in the room where they were.
When, after a little while, Yin inquired about the cause of
her death, Cheng said, 'Killed by dogs'. Yin exclaimed, 'How
could dogs kill a human being?' Cheng replied, 'She was not
human'. Yin cried in astonishment, 'Not human? What
then?' Cheng then told Yin how he had first met Miss Jen
and how she had come to her end, which Yin heard with
amazement, sighing repeatedly. The next day Yin and Cheng

set out in a carriage for Ma-wei, where they unearthed and inspected Miss Jen's remains before returning to Ch'ang-an in great sorrow. And they thought of past events and recalled that she differed from human beings in only one respect: she would not make her own clothes but bought them ready-made.

Later, Cheng was made Chief Groom of the Imperial Stables and became very rich, keeping himself a stable of a dozen horses. He died at the age of sixty-five. In the middle (early 770s) of the Ta-li reign, I, Shen Chi-chi, lived in Chung-ling (i.e. Tsinsien in Kiangsi Province) and was a friend of Yin, who spoke repeatedly about these events, so that I knew them well. Afterwards Yin became an Assistant Censor and concurrently Prefect of Lung-chou (i.e. parts of Shensi and Kansu provinces), dying at his post.

Alas, the feelings of sub-human creatures are not unlike those of men! Not to yield her Chastity to brute force, and sacrificing her life so as to please her beloved—these are acts surpassing some women of the present age. It is a pity that Master Cheng was not a man of greater discernment, that he loved her beauty but did not seek to ascertain her true disposition. A man of knowledge and judgment would not have been able to learn from such a one the principles of metamorphosis and the relation between spirit and matter, and expressed it all in writing, thus preserving her fine sentiments instead of being satisfied with the enjoyment of female charm. What a pity!

In the second year (781) of the Chien-chung reign, I was banished from my post as a Reminder to the south-east along with General P'ei Chi of the Guards, Deputy Prefect of the Metropolitan District Sun Ch'eng, Assistant Secretary of the Board of Revenue and Population Ts'ui Hsü, and Reminder Lu Ch'un. From Ch'ang-an to Wu (i.e. Kiangsu and Chekiang provinces) we travelled together by land and by boat. The Former Reminder Chu Fang, who was travelling privately, also came with us. Thus we floated together on the rivers Ying and Huai, and as our boats sped on, we feasted in the day and conversed at night, each telling of some strange adventure. When the various gentlemen heard the story of Miss Jen, they were all deeply moved and asked me to record it.

1. to conceal the tail that sometimes obtruded despite the fox's power of transformation.
2. a fictitious prefecture.
3. Lochwan, to the north of Ch'ang-an (Sien), is some considerable distance from Ma-wei, which is west of the capital.

''Twixt Soul and Body'

In the short section 'The Soul' (c. 358) of *T'ai-p'ing kuang-chi* there are two or three similar tales, in which the soul, obsessed with the beloved person, leaves the body behind to follow the cherished one. In the early tale 'P'ang O' (c. 358), the hero, P'ang O, a handsome man of Ningtsin (in Hopeh Province), pays a visit to the Shih family, whose daughter, peeping at him from within, is instantly attracted to him. Miss Shih is then seen to visit P'ang, whereupon P'ang's jealous wife has her bound and sent back to her home escorted by a maid. On the way Miss Shih melts into air and disappears. On the next occasion, P'ang's wife herself seizes Miss Shih and escorts her home. The Shih family insist that their daughter has not left the house, and when she is summoned, the bound girl disappears. Miss Shih now confesses that she has been visiting P'ang in her dreams. And the story-writer comments : 'For where the feelings are deeply stirred, the soul becomes their manifestation'. Miss Shih then refuses to take a husband. But after some time P'ang's wife dies of illness, and P'ang marries Miss Shih (p. 2830).

In 'The Student Cheng' (c. 358), a dead grandmother on the outskirts of Chengchow (in Honan Province) marries the soul of her maternal granddaughter to the hero. He then brings her back to her parents in Hwaiyin (i.e. Tsingkiang in Kiangsu Province), being careful to send word in advance.

E

The intelligence is greeted with astonishment and dismay, for the mother fears that the bride is her husband's daughter by some other wife, their own daughter having always been in the house. A servant is dispatched to look at the lady, who is the exact likeness of the young mistress at home. When, finally, the wandering spirit descends from the carriage and steps into the courtyard, the stay-at-home greets her, and soul and body merge (p. 2834).

In 'Wei Yin' (c. 358), a husband sent on a mission to Korea is joined on his journey by his wife's soul. When, two years later, they return, her soul is united again with her body, which had remained behind with her parents (p. 2834).

'Twixt Soul and Body' is in *T'ang-jen hsiao-shuo*, p. 49, and *T'ai-p'ing kuang-chi*, c. 358, pp. 2831–2, where it is entitled 'Wang Chou'. The three tales summarised above may also be found in *T'ang-jen hsiao-shuo*, pp. 50–1.

The story of 'Twixt Soul and Body' forms the plot of the Yüan play *Ch'ien-nü li-hun* ('Ch'ien-nü's Disembodied Soul') by Cheng Te-hui in *Yüan-ch'ü hsüan*, Wen-hsüeh ku-chi ed., pp. 705–19.

Ch'en Hsüan-yu, the author of 'Twixt Soul and Body', lived in the eighth century and seems only to be known in connection with our tale.

'Twixt Soul and Body

In the third year (692) of the T'ien-shou reign, having been appointed to a post in Heng-chou (i.e. Hengyang in Hunan Province), Chang I of Tsingho (in Hopeh Province), moved his family there. Chang was of a solitary disposition with few intimate friends. He had no sons, and of his two daughters, the elder one had died early, while the younger one, Dimple, was exceedingly beautiful. Chang had a nephew, Wang Chou of Taiyuan (in Shansi Province), who as a boy was clever as well as handsome, and for whom Chang had a high regard, often saying, 'One of these days I shall marry Dimple to him'. When Chou and Dimple grew up, they were filled with longing for each other without the family's knowledge. Then, later, one of Chang's colleagues, who was being considered for promotion by the Board of Civil Service, sought the hand of Dimple, and Chang gave his consent. When his daughter learned about it, she was greatly distressed, and Chou, too, being deeply resentful, thereupon announced his departure, stating that he was going to the capital to seek office. Unable to stop him, Chang conferred on him generous presents; and Chou, full of chagrin, bade the family farewell and boarded his boat.

By dusk he had reached a mountain village several *li* away. At midnight, unable to sleep, Chou heard the hurried footsteps of someone approaching the boat, which turned out to be Dimple walking in her bare feet. Mad with joy, Chou held her by the hand, asking how she had come. Dimple said, weeping, 'Such was your love for me that I could feel it even in my sleep and in my dreams. And now the family would have me change my course and renounce my true allegiance. But, being certain of your deep devotion, I was ready to lay down my life for you. And so I have run away from home to you'. Overjoyed at Dimple's coming, which was beyond his wildest hope, Chou hid her in the boat and immediately hoisted sail. Travelling at redoubled speed, they reached Szechwan after several months.

There they lived for the next five years, during which Dimple gave birth to two sons. And Chou would not send word to Chang about their whereabouts, but Dimple, who often thought of her parents, one day said, weeping, to Chou, 'Out of loyalty to you I neglected a daughter's duty and forsook my parents, from whom I have been estranged these five years. Deriving my breath from them, as from heaven and earth, I am thoroughly ashamed of my selfish happiness'. Moved by her words, Chou said, 'We shall at once return to them. Do not reproach yourself'. And together they made their return journey. On reaching Heng-Chou, Chou went ahead by himself to make his apology to his uncle and aunt. Chang, much surprised, said, 'But Dimple has been ill in her room these many years. What wayward talk is this?' Chou insisting that Dimple was in the boat, Chang, startled, sent a servant to investigate; and the servant found Dimple in the boat, glowing with health, and eagerly asking after the welfare of her parents, whereupon, dumbfounded, he hastily returned to report to Chang. When, with visible joy, the sick girl in the room heard the news, she rose from her bed, adorned herself and changed into new clothes. Then, smiling without uttering a word, she came out of her room to greet the other Dimple, their bodies merging into one with duplicated garments.

And the family regarded the affair as not in accordance

with what was right and proper, and kept it secret, notwith-standing which, there were some among their relatives who came to know about it. In the ensuing forty years, Chou and Dimple both died and their two sons both passed their examinations and held office as Assistant Magistrates. I, Ch'en Hsüan-yu, first heard the story in my youth, and there were several versions of it, though by some it was dismissed as pure fabrication. Then, towards the end (late 770s) of the Ta'li reign I met the Magistrate of Laiwu (in Shantung Province), Chang Chung-hsien,[1] who told me the story in detail. Chang Chung-hsien being a great nephew of Chang I, and his version the fullest, I now record it.

1. The character (i.e. ideograph) is not in the dictionaries, and I am assuming its pronunciation to be 'hsien'.

'The Beldame Feng'

The benighted traveller finding shelter in a tomb and
hospitably entertained by its ghost inmates is a common
theme in Chinese tales. In the section 'Ghost' (c. 316–c. 355)
in *T'ai-p'ing kuang-chi*, there are the following examples. In
'Ch'en A-teng' (c. 316, p. 2504), the traveller spends the
night in the tomb of a young girl, who invites a neighbour
in to be her chaperon. In the early tale 'Lu Chi' (c. 318,
p. 2514), the poet Lu Chi finds shelter in the tomb of the
philosopher Wang Pi. In the early tales 'Ch'in Shu' (c. 324,
p. 2568) and 'Chang-sun Shao-tsu' (c. 326, pp. 2586–7), the
traveller is treated to stale and tasteless food but enjoys the
favours of the woman ghost. In the probably early 'Wu
Hsiang' (c. 317, p. 2505), the female ghost also provides food
but dwells in a dilapidated house. In 'Tu-ku Mu' (c. 342,
pp. 2709–13), the hero is a descendant of a loyal general of
the Sui dynasty, and the ghost of a Princess of the Sui ruling
house sees fit to reward him and asks him to reinter her
remains. In 'Ts'ui Lo-shih' (c. 326, pp. 2588–9), the hero is
met by the ghost of the daughter of Wu Chih, a courtier of
the Three Kingdoms period, in her tomb. In 'T'ang Chien'
(c. 327, pp. 2599–600), T'ang Chien meets the ghost of a
woman about to be reburied with her husband and parents-
in-law. In 'Cheng Wang' (c. 336, p. 2668), Cheng Wang is
entertained by the ghost of a general in his tomb. And in

'the student Li of Hsün-yang' (c. 339, p. 2694), the hero spends the night in the tomb of a Miss Ts'ui, who declines an invitation to pass the evening with a ghost friend in order to guard over her guest.

The situation in 'The Beldame Feng' is paralleled in three tales in particular. In the early tale 'Chang Yü' (c. 318, pp. 2517–18), the traveller is entertained in a marsh near Tsingfeng (in Honan Province) by a woman of thirty odd with a train of maids. She informs him that she is a ghost and, weeping, tells her story. She was the daughter of a Prefect, and had two children by her husband, a son of eleven and a daughter of seven. After her death, her husband took one of her maids as his wife, so that her son is now constantly beaten by the stepmother. In the early tale 'Hsieh Miao-chih' (c. 318, pp. 2520–1), the ghost of a boy of ten is seen weeping in a tomb for distress at the idea of his mother remarrying, while the ghost of his father tries unavailingly to console him. Similarly, in 'Li Tso-wen' (c. 347, pp. 2751–2), a father and his young daughter, aged eight or so, are found in a tomb, with the child howling all through the night at the thought of its mother remarrying. In the last two tales, the mother learns on the following day of the anguish witnessed by the traveller, and abandons her intention of marrying again.

'The Beldame Feng' is in *T'ang-jen hsiao-shuo*, p. 98, and *T'ai-p'ing kuang-chi*, c. 343, pp. 2718–9.

Li Kung-tso, who wrote 'The Beldame Feng' was from Kansu Province and, by his own account, a Civil Administrative Officer of the Region between the Yangtze and the Huai in the early ninth century, travelling extensively in the region and further south in this, and probably a similar earlier and later, capacity. But his literary eminence considerably surpassed his official position. He is the author of three other extant tales, including 'The Prefect of Nan-k'o' (*T'ang-jen hsiao-shuo*, pp. 85–90).

The Beldame Feng

The Beldame Feng was the widow of a farm labourer in a village in Lukiang (in Anhwei Province). Being poor and without children, she was despised by her fellow-villagers and lived on her own. In the fourth year (809) of the Yüan-ho reign, a famine having broken out in the Huai and Ch'u regions (i.e. Anhwei, Kiangsu, Hupeh and Hunan provinces), Beldame Feng sought relief in Shu-chun (i.e. Tsienshan). Benighted on her way there at Mu-tu-shu, while standing under a mulberry tree to take refuge from the wind and rain, she suddenly saw the bright light in a roadside house and went towards it to seek shelter for the night. There she saw a beautiful and elegantly dressed woman of twenty odd with a three-year-old girl, both weeping bitterly by the door. Upon entering the house, the beldame saw also an old man and woman, both seated on the bed, gloomy and sullen in expression. The old couple whispered continually in each other's ears, and had the appearance of creditors chasing after bad debts; but when they saw Beldame Feng enter, they left the room without saying a word. After weeping by the door for some time, the young woman at last desisted and, coming back into the house, prepared the food and made the bed, inviting the beldame to eat and rest.

When the beldame asked her hostess why she had been crying, she again burst into tears, saying, 'The father of this girl is my husband. But tomorrow he will take another wife'. The beldame then asked who the old couple were, and why they seemed to be so angry, and what they wanted from her. She replied, 'They are my parents-in-law, who are demanding from me, now that their son is about to remarry, the various household articles and ritual vessels, which they will hand over to the new wife and from which I could not bear to be parted; hence their upbraiding'. In reply to the beldame's question as to where her husband was, the woman said, 'I am the daughter of Liang Ch'ien, Magistrate of Hwaiyin (i.e. Tsingkiang in Kiangsu Province), and have been married into the Tung family for seven years, bearing two sons and a daughter. The daughter is here, and the sons are with their father Tung Chiang, in the county town, where he is Assistant Magistrate[1] and enjoys great wealth'. And as she spoke, she continued to sob and choke. The beldame was no longer surprised and, having suffered from hunger and cold for many days, proceeded without further ado to eat of the dishes laid before her and then to rest herself.

The young woman continued to weep until dawn, when the beldame took her leave. After walking twenty *li*, she reached the county town of Tungcheng. In the eastern part of the town was a mansion decorated with many hangings, with sumptuous wedding gifts on display, round which people bustled about, saying, 'Tonight an official will celebrate his nuptials'. When the beldame asked who the bridegroom was, they told her it was Tung Chiang, whereupon she remarked, 'Tung has a wife. Why is he marrying again?' And a man from the county said, 'His wife and daughter are dead'. The beldame then said, 'Last night I was caught in the rain and slept in the house of Mrs Tung from the Liang family. How could she be dead?' When the man inquired where she had stopped for the night, the spot turned out to be the site of Mrs Tung's grave. The beldame then told about the old couple she had seen there, and they were the likeness of Tung Chiang's dead father and mother.

Tung Chiang, who was originally from Shu-chou, was known to all in the vicinity. Someone then apprising Tung of Beldame Feng's experience, Tung threatened to punish her as a witch, and ordered his followers to drive her away. The beldame then relating all that had happened to the men of the county, all who heard her account were much affected and broke into sighs. But that night, the wedding duly took place.

In the fifth month of the sixth year (811) of the Yüan-ho reign, the Civil Administrative Officer of the Region between the Yangtze and the Huai, Li Kung-tso, who had been sent on a mission to the capital, stayed at Han-nan (i.e. Icheng in Hupeh Province) on his return journey. In the government hostel there he met Kao Yüeh of Po-hai (i.e. Pinhsien in Shantung Province), Chao Tsan of Tienshui (in Kansu Province) and Yü-wen Ting of Loyang. In the evening they recounted, for each other's benefit, marvellous events they had heard about. Kao Yüeh told the story about the beldame Feng, and I, Li Kung-tso, recorded this account of her.

1. The original reads : 'Assistant Magistrate of Tsan', but this could be an error or mere fiction, since the county of Tsan, near Chuantsiao, 150 km north-east of Tungcheng, had been abolished before the T'ang.

'The Carp'

Among the tales in the section 'Creatures of the Water' (c. 464–c. 472) in *T'ai-p'ing kuang-chi*, there are a number in which a man is transformed into a fish, or a fish into a man. In an early tale, Kun, father of the great Yü, tamer of floods, after nine years' unsuccessful efforts to control the flood waters, drowns himself in Feather Pool and is transformed into a black fish ('Kun of Hsia', c. 466, p. 3837). In another early tale 'Lazy Woman Fish' (c. 465, p. 3836), the fish derives its name from a lazy daughter-in-law who, in order to escape the ire of her mother-in-law, drowns herself and becomes a fish. In 'Wei Sheng-liang' (c. 469, pp. 3863–4), quoting an early account, a white fish, three feet in length, caught by a fisherman turns into a woman and becomes the fisherman's wife. And in the probably early 'Wang Su' (c. 468, p. 3856), a white fish transformed into a man seeks the hand of the daughter of the Wang family.

The carp enjoyed a special position among fish. It was rated a delicacy and considered to possess magical properties. Its name 'li', which is derived from the regularity of the pattern formed by its scales, is a homophone of the surname 'Li', which was the surname of the ruling house of the T'ang dynasty, for which reason for some time in the T'ang the eating of carp was forbidden, all carp caught being required by law to be set free again (*Yu-yang tsa-tsu*, c. 17, Ts'ung-shu

chi-ch'eng ed., c. 6, p. 137). The carp was associated with the
dragon, which was thought sometimes to adopt the guise of
a carp, as in this poem by Emperor Yang of the Sui:

> On the third of the third month I stand facing the river
> And see the carp sporting among the waves.
> I would fain lower my rod and catch a few,
> But desist for fear they may be dragons.

> (Quoted in *Ku-chin t'u-shu chi-ch'eng*, XIX, c. 139,
> 'The Carp', Literary Compositions, p. 1b)

In 'Old Woman of Fen-shui' in the section 'The Dragon' in
T'ai-p'ing kuang-chi, c. 424, pp. 3453–4, a red carp caught by
an old woman and kept in a pond changes into a dragon
which leaves a large pearl as a gift for its benefactress. And
in 'Ts'ui Tao-shu' (c. 423, pp. 3445–6), a golden carp, five
feet long, caught in a well and cooked and eaten, turns out
to have been a dragon, so that punishment is visited upon
those feasting on it. And in the Ming novel *Hsi-yu chi*,
Chapter IX, the top graduate Ch'en Kuang-jui sets free a
golden carp that is actually the Dragon King (Tso-chia ed.,
pp. 90–2).

'Dragon's Gate' in *T'ai-p'ing kuang-chi*, c. 466, records the
tradition that the carp swarm up the Yellow River in late
spring and try to leap up the gorge known as 'Dragon's Gate',
those succeeding in making the leap being transformed into
dragons (p. 3839). In 'Man of Chiang-chou' (c. 471, p. 3881),
which was probably based on an early account, a man aged
over a hundred grows horns and is later transformed into a
carp, though returning at intervals in human guise to his
family. Similarly, in the early tale 'A Single Horn' (c. 471,
p. 3881), a man several hundred years old grows a single
horn and becomes a carp. And in the probably early 'Tzu
Ying-ch'un' (c. 467, pp. 3546–7), a red carp ascends to
heaven, carrying its benefactor on its back.

But the cast of mind in our tale is really Buddhist and the
dominant idea, the transmigration of the soul, Indian in
origin. The Buddhist moral is more pronounced in a briefer

and probably earlier version of the story, entitled 'Chang Tsung' under the section 'Retribution' in *T'ai-p'ing kuang-chi*, c.132. The hero Chang Tsung, Police Officer of Tsinkiang (in Fukien Province), who is fond of eating minced fish, falls ill and dies, then revives after seven days. While he lies dead, an official of the underworld suggests that, in view of his indulgence, he ought to be punished by becoming a fish, whereupon Chang's soul is pushed into a river and changed into a tiny fish, growing in seven days into a carp over two feet in length. The carp is then caught in a fisherman's net. An attendant sent by Chang's colleague, Wang, in the local county office to buy fish is fobbed off with a small catch by the fisherman but, after having been caned by his superior, returns to find the carp among the rushes, which he takes back to Wang's house. In the parlour Wang's wife is making her toilet and has one arm bare. In the kitchen the cook removes the scales of the carp with his knife, and then beheads it. Thereupon Chang revives. At the news of Chang's revival, another colleague hurries away from a meal of minced fish to Chang's bedside. Chang then grasps his hand and asks whether he has enjoyed his dish of minced fish (pp. 942–3). The tale may also be found on p. 228 of *T'ang-jen hsiao-shuo*.

And in the early tale 'Yüan Chih-tsung' (c.131), a man fond of hunting and fishing dies for an evening, during which he is taken to hell, where his skin is flayed and his flesh cut up, after which he is thrown into water and drawn out with a hook in his mouth, slit open and sliced; he is then, in turn, boiled and roasted over an oven (pp. 928–9).

The Lord of the River already occurs in *Chuang-tzu*, Book XVII, 'Autumn Floods'. And in the early tale 'Ko Hsüan' (c. 466, p. 3839), a fish brings a letter to, and from, the Lord of the River.

'The Carp' is in *T'ang-jen hsiao-shuo*, pp. 225–7, and *T'ai-p'ing kuang-chi*, c. 471, pp. 3881–3, both under the title 'Hsüeh Wei'.

'The Carp' and the three following tales formed part of the collection 'More Tales about the Mysterious and Strange', written in the second quarter of the ninth century by Li Fu-yen, who, by his own account, was from Kansu Province.

The Carp

In the first year (758) of the Ch'ien-yüan reign, Hsüeh Wei was Keeper of Archives of Ch'ing-ch'eng County in Shu-chou (near Kwanhsien in Szechwan Province) and had, as colleagues, Assistant Magistrate Tsou P'ang and Police Officers Lei Chi and P'ei Liao. In the autumn of that year, Wei was taken ill, and at the end of seven days, seemed to have expired. All efforts to awaken him met with no response, but there was a patch still warm round his heart, and his family could not bear to proceed with funeral ceremonies, but crowded instead round his bed, watching him. After twenty days, the dead man heaved a sigh, and, sitting up, asked those near him, 'How many days have elapsed in the world?' When they replied, 'Twenty days', Hsüeh then said, 'Will someone go and see if my colleagues are having minced fish? Let them know I have revived; and ask them to stop eating and come to listen to my strange story'. A servant sent to observe the officials found them about to fall to a dish of minced fish, and immediately conveyed Hsüeh's request, whereupon they stopped eating and came to him.

Hsüeh said to his assembled colleagues, 'Did you gentlemen order the attendant Chang Pi to buy some fish?' When they replied that they had done so, Hsüeh sent for Chang and said to him, 'Hiding a large carp, the fisherman Chao Kan sold smaller fish to his customers. But you found the hidden

fish when you looked among the rushes, and brought it
back with you. And as you entered the county court, the
Clerk of Population was sitting to the east of the gate and
the Clerk of Litigation to the west, having a game of chess.
When you came up the steps, Assistant Magistrate Tsou and
Police Officer Lei were playing dice, and Police Officer P'ei
eating a peach, and when you then related how the fisherman
had hidden the large carp, P'ei said that the man ought to be
given a thrashing. You then gave the fish to the cook Wang
Shih-liang, who received it with great satisfaction before
killing it'. And the company demanded of one another what
they had been doing and saying, and it had all been as in
Hsüeh's account. The others thereupon asking Hsüeh how
he came to know these things, Hsüeh answered, 'I was the
carp that was killed in the kitchen'. His colleagues, astounded,
begged him to explain himself.

Hsüeh said, 'At first, as I lay ill, I was much troubled by
the heat, which was almost unbearable. Then I dreamt, and
in my dream I forgot I was ill, but still longing to escape
from the stifling heat, took a stick with me and went out.
When I left the city's outer wall, my heart was filled with
gladness, and my sense of deliverance like that of a caged
bird or animal set free. I wandered into the mountains,
whence, again feeling smothered, I made my way down to
the river bank. The clear water in the deep river[1] was the
hue of the autumn sky, and being still and like a mirror,
reflected distant ephemeral scenes. I was suddenly impelled
by the desire to disport myself in water, and taking off my
clothes, jumped into the stream. As a child I had been keen
on swimming, though I had since given up the exercise, but
with the release of my body, I now recaptured old longings,
and childhood delights. I said involuntarily, "A swimmer
cannot equal the felicitous motion of fish. If for a brief
interval I could take on the form of a fish and achieve the
ultimate in swimming!" A fish near by heard me and said,
"I do not think that you will really want that. It is easy to

gain the existence of a fish, and much more to adopt a transitory guise as one. I will attend to the matter." And the fish swam resolutely away.

'Before long, a human figure several feet in height, with a fish-head for its crown, riding on a whale and leading a procession of dozens of fish, approached and read out the proclamation of the Lord of the River: "The ways of men and fish differ, the one dwelling in towns, the other in water, the two remaining apart except when there is real affinity between them. We have taken cognizance of the expressed inclination of the Keeper of Archives Hsüeh to enjoy an unfettered existence afloat in the deep. Delighting in the wide expanse of the watery sphere, he has consigned his cares to the clear river; tired of mountain scenes, he is renouncing his office in the world of illusion. Accordingly we sanction his transformation, temporary and not lasting, into a fish and appoint him, for a period only, the Red Carp of the Eastern Pool. He must, however, be warned, that to overturn boats by taking advantage of the force of the current is to incur blame in secret, and that to be enticed by the bait and brave the hook is to injure oneself in the open. Let him not endanger himself and earn the opprobrium of his fellows."

'I had no sooner heard the proclamation than I found myself transformed into a fish. Giving way to every momentary impulse, I swam at will amidst the waves as well as at the bottom of the pool, going wherever I liked; and I roamed all over the Three Rivers and the Five Lakes, returning every evening to the Eastern Pool, where I was stationed. Then, one day, feeling hungry and unable to find food, I followed in the wake of a boat and suddenly saw the fisherman Chao Kan lowering his rod with a tempting bait at the end of the line. As I drew near the bait, I warned myself, saying, "I am a man and, only for the time being, a fish. Though I have not eaten, I must not bite the hook", and I swam away from the bait. Presently, my hunger growing acute, I thought to myself, "I am an official whom a moment's

F

fancy has changed into a fish, so that even if I swallowed the bait, the fisherman would not dare kill me but only send me back to the county offices." So I snapped at the bait, whereupon the fisherman retracted the line. When I was about to fall into his hands, I called out repeatedly to Chao Kan, who ignored my cry, and putting a cord through my gills, hid me among the rushes.

'Then I heard Chang Pi arrive and bawl out, "Police Officer P'ei wants a fish, a large one." Chao Kan replied, "I have not got a large one, sir, only a dozen catties of small ones."[2] Undeterred, Chang countered, "Small ones would not do; my orders are to buy a large fish", and searching among the rushes, found me and took me away. So I shouted out to Chang, "Show respect for your superiors, man! I am the Keeper of Archives of the county, only a fish in disguise." Paying no heed to my words, Chang continued to carry me in his hand even when I went on to scold him, which made no impression. We entered through the gate of the county court, where I saw the Clerks sitting and playing chess, and when I called out aloud to them, they never responded but only said, "A fearful size! The carp must weigh four catties!" When we ascended the steps, Tsou and Lei, who were playing a game of dice, and P'ei, who was eating a peach, were all pleased to see such a large fish and ordered it to be dressed for dinner. And Chang told how Chao Kan had hidden the carp, whereupon P'ei said angrily that the fisherman ought to be thrashed. I then shouted aloud to you gentlemen in desperation, "You are about to kill me, your colleague! You will not spare even *me* in your haste to gorge yourselves. What kind of humanity is this?" But my shouting and weeping produced not the slightest effect on the three of you, and I was handed over to the cook Wang Shih-liang, who had been sharpening a knife and who laid me with alacrity on a table. I called out, "Wang, remember you are my cook. Why do you want to kill me? Why do you not tell the gentlemen who I am?" But seeming not to hear me, Wang placed my neck on the chopping board and beheaded me, and with the rolling off of my head in the kitchen, I regained consciousness here. And it was then that I sent for you'.

The company being profoundly amazed, feelings of compassion were born in their hearts. For when the fisherman caught the fish, when the attendant held it, when the clerks were at their chess game, when the three colleagues were at the top of the steps, when the cook was about to kill it, they all saw the mouth of the fish move but never heard a sound. Thereupon the three colleagues abstained from the minced fish and forswore the dish all their lives. Hsüeh Wei was well from then on, being later appointed Assistant Magistrate of Hua-yang near Changtu in Szechwan Province before he died.

1. The river would be the Min-kiang, a tributary of the Yangtze.
2. Petty officials were not always good customers, demanding the best but often refusing to pay a fair price for it. Hence the fisherman's reluctance to produce the carp.

'Rain-making'

Tung Chung-shu (176 B.C.–105 B.C.) extending the idea of the sacrifice for rain in The Annals of Spring and Autumn, had clay dragons set up to pray for rain, reasoning that clouds and dragons keep each other company, since it is stated in The Book of Changes: 'Clouds follow the dragon; the wind follows the tiger'. Inasmuch, then, as affinity governs all that exists, so the setting up of clay dragons would, it thus follows, give rise to clouds and rain.

The quotation is from the chapter 'Dragons Investigated' in *Lun-heng* (Ssu-pu ts'ung-k'an ed., c.16, p.1a) by the later Han philosopher Wang Ch'ung (see also the chapter 'Praying for Rain' in Tung Chung-shu's *Ch'un-ch'iu fan-lu*, Ssu-pu ts'ung-k'an ed., c.16, pp. 3a–6a). Thus the belief in the dragon's faculty of making rain began at least as early as the Han dynasty and was not merely held by the populace.

In our tale, the hero Li Ching chances upon a Dragons' Palace in the Huo Mountains. In the tale 'Liu I' pays a visit to the Dragon King in his ornate palace in Tungting Lake, and also meets the King's choleric brother, the Lord of the Ch'ien-t'ang river, whose thunderous bawling thoroughly frightens him. Earlier, Liu meets the Dragon King's daughter in the guise of a young woman tending sheep, which are then found to be not sheep but clouds, which she calls 'rain-workers' (see General Introduction, p. 17, *supra* *T'ai-p'ing kuang-chi*, c. 419, pp. 3410–7).

In other tales in the section 'The Dragon' (c. 418–c. 425) in *T'ai-p'ing kuang-chi*, dragons make rain. 'Dragon Burial Ground' (c. 418, p. 3403) endorses early tradition that mountains and hills with dragons buried under them are able to influence the weather and bring rain. In the early tale 'Kan Tsung' (c. 418, p. 3402), a foreign magician would carry dragons, reduced in size to a few inches in length, to places suffering from drought and the dragons would bring rain (see Wang Ming (ed.), *Pao-p'u-tzu nei-p'ien chiao-shih*, Appendix I, p. 328). In 'Hsiao Hsin' (c. 421, p. 3426), a monk conjures up a dragon and a great downpour. In 'Tamer of Dragons' (c. 423, p. 3443), a 'tamer of dragons' causes a black dragon inhabiting a pond to make rain, but this results in a flooding of the Han river, in which thousands are drowned. In 'The Monk Hsüan-chao' (c. 420, pp. 3419–20), when the monk asks his dragon-disciples to make rain and alleviate the drought, they reply that it is easy enough to gather the clouds and send rain, but that arbitrarily causing rain to fall is strictly prohibited by heaven. In the early tale 'The Sick Dragon', the rain supplied by the ailing dragon has a stench (see General Introduction, p. 10, *supra*). And in the Ming novel *Hsi-yu chi*, Chapter 10, the Dragon King is punished by decapitation for not complying strictly with the orders of the Emperor of Heaven regarding the hour and the amount of the rain allowed to fall (Tso-chia ed., pp. 105–10).

The Huo Mountains (Hwo-shan) to the east of Hwohsien (in Shansi Province), one of the four minor holy mountains, seem to have no particular association with dragons except in our tale.

Li Ching, Duke of Wei (571–649), a famous general of the early T'ang, who began as an official in the Sui dynasty, was gifted both as a military strategist and as an administrator. His charm and magnetic personality are commemorated in the tale 'The Curly-bearded Stranger' by

Tu Kuang-t'ing (850–933) (*T'ang-jen hsiao-shuo*, pp.178–181). Our story is incorporated in Chapter 3 of the historical narrative, *Sui T'ang yen-i*, by Ch'u Jen-huo of the early Ch'ing (Ku-tien ed., pp. 20–2). But in the more popular narrative, *Shuo T'ang* (ed. Ch'en Ju-heng, Chung-hua 1959, Chapter 12, p. 54), Li Ching is portrayed as a wizard able to soar with the clouds and command the elements. The cryptic remarks about vassalage at the end of our story would refer to Li Ching's subsequent allegiance to the T'ang Emperors.

The saying 'Generals come from west of the Pass, but Prime Ministers from east of it' is to be found in *Hou-Han shu*, punctuated ed., c. 58, p.1866, where generals and Prime Ministers of the Ch'in and the Han from west and east of the Pass (i.e. Han-ku Pass near Lingpao in Honan Province, about 55 kilometres east of Tungkwan) are listed in the Commentary. By 'west of the Pass' are meant Shensi and Kansu provinces; and by 'east of the Pass', Shansi, Honan, Shantung and Hopeh provinces. Li Ching was from Sanyuan (in Shensi Province), which is west of the Pass.

'Rain-making' is in *T'ang-jen hsiao-shuo*, pp. 228–30, and *T'ai-p'ing kuang-chi*, c. 418, pp. 3407–9. Its author was Li Fu-yen of the ninth century.

Rain Making

When Li Ching, Duke of Wei, was still a commoner, he often hunted in the Huo Mountains (in Shansi Province), finding shelter and refreshment in a mountain village, one of whose elders, struck by Li's appearance and manner, was wont to present him with gifts of food, increasing with the years. On one occasion, while in pursuit of a herd of deer late in the afternoon, being unwilling to forgo his prey, he lost his bearings in the dark and could not find his way back. Balked of his hopes, he plodded on wearily, when suddenly catching sight of a lamp in the distance, he rushed towards it and found a stately residence with a red gate and high walls. After knocking on the gate for a long time, when someone came out to ask what he wanted, Li said that he had lost his way and begged for a night's lodging. The man said, 'Both the gentlemen are away, only the old lady is at home. A night's lodging is out of the question'. When Li, nevertheless, asked the man to inquire for him, the man went in and, coming out again soon afterwards, said, 'Our mistress would not agree at first, but seeing it is a dark night and you have lost your way, she has decided to offer you hospitality'. Li was then invited into the parlour.

After some time, a maidservant came and announced her mistress, who turned out to be a woman aged fifty and over, in a green skirt and a plain white jacket, with an air of

refinement as became the lady of a great household. Stepping
forward, Li bowed to her, who bowed in return, saying, 'My
sons are both away, and I ought not to have detained you.
But, since it is dark and you do not know your way, if I
turned you out, where could you go? I have to tell you
though, that this is a house of rude villagers. My sons may
return at any moment and you must excuse their loud
bawling, nor let it frighten you'. Li said, 'How should I
dare?' Presently a meal was served, and the viands were
tasty with a preponderance of fish. When Li had stopped
eating, the lady retired and two maids brought a bed, mats
and bedding, the quilt being clean and scented, and all else
choice and sumptuous. Having made the bed, the maids shut
the door and fastened it, and Li, left to himself, began to
wonder what the inmates of the house might be, for to return
by night to a home in the wilds and bawl loudly would seem
to suggest spirits. Seized by fear, Li durst not go to sleep
but sat up and waited.

Towards midnight, he heard a loud knocking at the gate
and, when someone had answered it, a ringing voice calling
out, 'Receive Heaven's command issued with this order tally.
The eldest son shall make rain, circumscribing these
mountains for seven hundred *li*, distribution of the appropriate
amount to be completed by the fifth watch without dilatori-
ness and with due care to avoid wreaking havoc'. The man
at the gate taking the tally and bringing it in to report, the
lady of the house was presently heard to say to the others,
'My two sons are not back yet. And now the order for rain
has come with this tally, for which there can be no evasion
and tardy execution of which would bring punishment. If I
sent for my sons, it would be too late; and the servants
cannot be entrusted with such a task. What shall we do?'
A young maid then said, 'Just then I had a look at the
gentleman in the parlour, who is certainly no common
personage. Why not ask him to do it?' Well-pleased with
the suggestion, the lady knocked on the parlour door herself,

saying, 'Is the gentleman awake? Would he please come out for a moment'. Li expressing assent, went down the steps to meet her, whereupon the lady said, 'Honoured guest, this is not a human dwelling but a Dragons' Palace. An order tally from Heaven for rain-making has come in the absence of my elder son, who has gone to a wedding in the Eastern Ocean, and of my younger, who is away escorting his sister on a journey. It is over ten thousand *li* to where my sons are, there is insufficient time to send for them, and in my predicament of having to find a substitute, I thought of you at this juncture. Would you be willing to carry out the task?' Li replied, 'I am but a poor mortal, not a god. How could I make rain? But if you will teach me how, I am ready to obey you'. The lady said, 'If you will only follow my instructions, it can easily be done'. And she first bade the steward bring the piebald horse and then ordered the rain vessel to be fetched, which was a small bottle to be tied to the saddle. She then gave Li these directions: 'When you ride, go easy on the bit and reins. Just let the horse pick its own way, and when it rears and neighs, take one drop of water from the bottle and place it on the mane. Be sure not to take more than a drop'.

Li mounted the horse, which soon left the ground and was afloat in the air, while he marvelled that his seat was so firm, hardly realizing that he was above the clouds. A terrific wind blew, and thunder roared beneath his feet. And whenever the horse reared, he put a drop of the water on its mane. After some time, there was a flash of lightning, and through the scattered clouds he saw below him the mountain village in which he was accustomed to find shelter. And he thought: 'Indebted, as I have been, to the kind hospitality of the villagers and at a loss as to how I could repay them, now that there has been a drought, with the crops dying, and I hold rain in my hands, I must not be niggardly in dispensing it'. And he considered that a drop was not enough to moisten the ground, and sprinkled twenty drops on the horse's mane.

Before very long, the rain-making being over, he returned on the horse to the Palace of the Dragons.

He was greeted by his hostess, who was weeping in the parlour, saying, 'How could you make such a mistake? I told you to dispense *one* drop. Why did you, out of gratitude to the villagers, dispense twenty? A drop in Heaven is the equivalent of ten inches of rain on earth, so that the village had twenty feet of rain in the middle of the night. And do you think that any of the inhabitants would still be alive? I have already been punished, having received eighty strokes of the rod, with my back full of blood-stained scars, and concerned, too, for my sons, who are also implicated. What have you got to say?' Filled with consternation, Li durst not reply.

The lady then said, 'Since you, sir, are a mortal, not acquainted with the mysteries of rain-making, I must absolve you from blame, but if the other dragons came after you, they would strike terror into your heart. You should now leave, but not before I have repaid you for your trouble. Here in these mountains all we can offer you is two slaves, of whom you can have both or only one, according to your inclination'. And she commanded that the two slaves be brought forward: one of them coming out of the eastern wing of the house, with a mild manner and pleasing countenance, wearing an expression of gladness; the other out of the western wing, raging with fury and standing there, the picture of anger. Li said, 'I am a hunter, accustomed to combat savage beasts. If I chose a pleasing slave, people would accuse me of cowardice'. He then said to her, 'I would not presume to accept both. Since you are so kind, I will accept the angry one'. The lady smiled and said, 'Let it be according to your wish'.

After bowing and bidding the lady farewell, Li left with his slave; and when they had taken a few paces, they looked back and found that the house had disappeared. Li then thought of questioning his slave, but the enraged creature having also disappeared, Li now found his way back by himself. It being soon dawn, he looked at the village and found it immersed in water, with only the tops of large trees jutting out. There was not a sign of any survivor.

Li Ching eventually pacified the land with his army, his achievement being greater than that of any other in the empire, but failed to become Prime Minister. Was this not foreshadowed in his rejection of the pleasing slave? It is said that Prime Ministers come from east of the Pass, but generals from west of it. Were east and west what the slaves portended? Certainly they betokened vassalage; only, if Li had accepted both slaves, he would have become both general and Prime Minister.

'The Tiger'

The transformation of a man into a tiger is a common theme in the section 'The Tiger' (c. 426–c. 433) in *T'ai-p'ing kuang-chi*. In the early tale 'Prefect Feng' (c. 426, p. 3466), Prefect Feng of Suancheng (in Kiangsi Province) turns into a tiger and devours the local inhabitants. The transformation is often brought about through the wearing of a tiger skin, as in 'The Taoist of Hsia-k'ou' (c. 426, pp. 3472–3) and 'Fei Chung' (c. 427, pp. 3474–5). In 'Candidate for Office in the T'ien-pao reign' (c. 427, p. 3479) and 'Shen-t'u Ch'eng' (c. 429, pp. 3486–8), the hero's wife is transformed into a tiger with the aid of a tiger skin. In 'Wang Chü-chen' (c. 430, p. 3495), the tiger skin is equally effectual in transformation when worn by another person. (And in the early tale 'Huan Ch'an', Huan Ch'an of Poyang (in Kiangsi Province) having incurred the wrath of the local deity by offering half-cooked sacrificial meat, is condemned to eat raw flesh and transformed into a tiger when a stripy skin is thrown over him; *I yüan*, Hsüeh-chin t'ao-yüan ed., c. 8, p. 11a.)

The transformation may be the result of illness, as in 'Petty Official of Ch'en-chou' (c. 426, pp. 3471–2), or of madness, as in the early tale 'Shih Tao-hsüan' (c. 426, p. 3468). In 'Li Cheng' (c. 427, pp. 3476–9; *T'ang-jen hsiao-shuo*, pp. 220–2), there is a long conversation between Li

Cheng, now a tiger, and his former friend Yüan Ts'an, in which the different stages of the transformation are described:

> In my former shape I travelled to Wu and Ch'u, returning only last year. My route lay across Ju-fen (near Yehsien in Honan Province), where I caught an illness and grew mad. I went into a mountain valley, and presently put my left and right hand down on the ground and treaded on all fours. Then I felt my heart become more cruel and my strength increase immensely. And then, when I looked at my arms and thighs, there was hair growing on them. And when I saw those clad in hat and raiment walking along the roads, or those loaded with burden hurrying on their way, or winged creatures taking to the air, or hairy animals scampering, I wanted to catch and devour them. (p. 3478; pp. 221-2)

Finally, the tiger dictates his complete works in nearly twenty chapters before parting from his friend.

In the early tale 'The Monk-tiger' (c. 433, pp. 3512 – 13), a monk in the mountains outside Ichun (in Kiangsi Province) in the habit of putting on a tiger skin to frighten passers-by and picking up the bundles they abandon, becomes a tiger when, one day, the skin sticks to his body. But after killing another monk, repentance brings about his reversion to human form. Subsequently he confesses his misdeeds to his master, who gives the following explanation to the transformation:

> Life and death, sin and blessing are all caused by thought . . . Your evil thought caused you to be transformed into a tiger, but your good thought caused you to become a monk again.

Our tale finds a parallel in 'Scholar of Nan-yang' (c. 432, pp. 3504 – 6; *T'ang-jen hsiao-shuo*, pp. 219 – 20), which is essentially the same story except for these features: there is a fore-warning of the transformation from a tiger messenger;

the transformation follows a period of illness; and the hero is
eventually killed by the son of his victim.

'The Tiger' is in *T'ang-jen hsiao-shuo*, pp. 218 – 19, and
T'ai-p'ing kuang-chi, c. 429, pp. 3490 –1. Its author was Li
Fu-yen of the ninth century.

The Tiger

Towards the end (804) of the Cheng-yüan reign, Chang Feng of Nanyang (in Honan Province) travelling to the regions south of the Pass, broke his journey at the inn under Transverse Mountain in Fu-t'ang County in Foochow Prefecture (i.e. Futsing in Fukien Province). It had just stopped raining, and the mountains displaying all their colours in the evening sun and a haze blending with the mists, Chang took his stick to go on a walk, and before realising it, had wandered very far. Coming upon a lawn of soft and lush grass, over a hundred paces in length and in breadth, beside a small tree, Chang took off his clothes, hanging them on the tree and laying his stick against it, threw himself upon the grass and rolled from left to right. Suddenly he fell fast asleep; and he dreamt that he was treading on all fours like an animal. Feeling satisfied with himself, he rose and found that he had changed into a tiger, marked with stripes on its skin and possessed of sharp claws and teeth and a powerful, muscular frame, indeed the king of beasts. So he jumped up and roamed over hill and dale, his motion swift as lightning.

It being now late into the night, he felt hungry and stalked near a village, but there was not a dog or pig or horse or calf to be had, and in the chaos of his mind the idea arose that he was to devour Secretary Cheng of Foochow Prefecture, and accordingly hid by the wayside. Before long a man coming from the south, who was an officer waiting to welcome Cheng, addressed another man saying, 'Secretary Cheng Fan is expected at the inn. Would you know when he started out?' The other man said, 'That is my master, whose luggage, I am told, has only just reached the inn'. The officer then asked, 'Is he travelling alone or has he got companions? When I greet him, I am so afraid that I might bow to the wrong person'. The lackey replied, 'There are three of them, among whom Master Cheng is the one clad in dark green'. All this while, Chang had been waiting, and having overheard the conversation, which seemed to have been for his benefit, hid himself in anticipation of Cheng's arrival. Presently Cheng did arrive, dressed in dark green, fat, and proud in his bearing, with a large train of attendants; and as soon as Cheng reached the place where the tiger had been hiding, it swooped upon him and, holding him in its mouth, went up a mountain. It being then not yet dawn and none of Cheng's followers venturing to give chase, unmolested, the tiger ate Cheng up, leaving only his hair and entrails. And the tiger then went prowling among the mountains and woods, being entirely on its own.

The tiger now thought, 'I, who was originally a man, cannot rejoice in being a tiger confined to these mountains. Why do I not seek out the spot where the transformation took place and resume the shape of a man again?' So he went in search of the place, which he came upon by sunset, finding his clothes still hanging on the tree, and the stick leaning against it; and the grass looking still lush and green, he rolled about on it. Then, feeling satisfied with himself, he rose and found that he had resumed his human form, whereupon he clad himself, took his stick and returned to the inn. He had been away for exactly one day.

When, on the previous day, Chang's servants lost sight of him, they learnt, on inquiry in the neighbourhood, that he had taken a stick and gone into the mountains, and went in search of him along the paths without success. Chang having now returned, they asked where he had been. And Chang lied to them, saying, 'I followed a torrent to a monastery in the mountains, where I discussed Buddhist doctrine with the monks until it was too late to return'. The servants said, 'Early this morning a tiger in the vicinity ate Secretary Cheng of Foochow Prefecture, whose remains have been sought in vain. There are savage beasts in these mountains and woods, of which the lone traveller has to be wary. Your failure to return yesterday caused us all great anxiety. Heaven be praised, you are now safely back'. Chang then resumed his travels.

In the sixth year (811) of the Yüan-ho reign, Chang travelled to Huai-yang (i.e. Tsingkiang of Kiangsu Province), staying at the government hostel. At a banquet given by the warden of the hostel, the guests played a drinking game, requiring the one upon whom the lot fell to relate some strange adventure, in which he himself had been involved, it being left to the company to punish a narrator whose adventure was not deemed strange enough. When the lot fell to Chang, he related the events at Transverse Mountain. Occupying the lowest seat was the higher graduate Cheng Hsia, the son of the same Secretary Cheng, who rose with eyes bulging in anger and, grasping a sword, threatened to kill Chang in revenge for his father's death. The other guests intervening and parting the two, Hsia would not be pacified and informed the Prefectural authorities, but was eventually persuaded to continue his journey to the south, the officers at the ferry strictly having been enjoined not to convey him back to Huai-yang. Chang was made to travel westwards and to change his name so as not to attract notice again. Some there are who maintain that a father's death must be avenged; but Cheng's death was not a deliberate act of murder, and if Hsia had killed Chang, he himself would still be punished by the law. Thus the parties were kept apart and the death remained unavenged.

G

'Old Chang'

There are some similar tales in the section 'Immortals' (c.1–c.55) in *T'ai-p'ing kuang-chi*. In 'Hermit of Heng-shan' (c.45, p.283), a mysterious medicine-vendor is able to afford the betrothal gift of five hundred strings of cash demanded by the parents of a beautiful girl, whose hand he gains. He and his wife are later visited in their celestial home by her parents.

In 'P'ei Ch'en' (c.17, pp.116–18), Wang Ching-po, a Judge of the Supreme Court, calls on his former hermit companion P'ei Ch'en, who pretends now to be a seller of medicines at the market, in 'a cherry orchard with a carriage gate' to the east of Green Garden Bridge outside Yangchow:

Ching-po had been in Yangchow for over ten days. When he had dealt with most of the official business, he remembered the words of his friend P'ei Ch'en and went out of the city to look for him. There indeed was a carriage gate and, when Ching-po inquired, it was the P'ei house. He was ushered in, and at first found it somewhat desolate, but with each few steps, the scenery improved. After several hundred paces, he reached the gate of the house. Towers and pavilions projected on all sides, and the trees and flowers were verdant and fresh. The scene seemed out of this world, it was so bright and lush, an indescribably delightful setting.

Fragrant breezes refreshed one's mind and spirits, as if
one were transported into the very heavens . . . Presently
was heard the sound of tinkling ornaments, and two
maidservants came out and announced 'Master P'ei'. A
figure then emerged, clad in majestic robes and hat, and
with a magnificent cast of features. Ching-po went
forward to bow and, on taking a look, saw that it *was*
P'ei. His host said soothingly, 'To be an official in this
dusty world, fed on rank flesh, consumed with earthly
desires—what a burdensome trip you have had!' (p.117)

Subsequently P'ei conjures up Ching-po's wife, who had been
left behind in the capital, to play on the zither for the
company.

In 'Lu and Li' (c.17, pp.118–19), the two students Lu and
Li both aspire to the existence of a recluse in the mountains.
Having abandoned the hermit life, Li later visits Lu, who has
succeeded in becoming an immortal, and finds Lu in regal
splendour in Yangchow. Lu then presents Li with a walking
stick, with which as token Li is to obtain twenty thousand
strings of cash from a Persian shop. And in 'Hsüeh Chao'
(c.17, pp.120–1), Ts'ui Yü abandons the hermit life to
become an official and later visits his former companion
Hsüeh Chao, who has become an immortal.

'Chang and Li' (c.23, p.158) is essentially the same tale
as 'Lu and Li' and 'P'ei Ch'en'. On the way to Yangchow,
Li meets his former hermit friend Chang. And Chang conjures
up Li's wife to play on the zither for the company. At their
parting, Chang presents Li with a straw hat with which to
claim three hundred thousand strings of cash from a herbalist's
shop owned by one Old Wang. The hat is identified by
Wang's daughter, who patched it with green thread some
years back.

As for the paraphernalia of the gods — phoenixes and cranes
as mounts, ascent and descent to the sound of music, fragrance
in the air — they are all to be found in the early tale 'Emperor
Wu of Han' (i.e. *Han Wu-ti nei-chuan*; c.3, pp.13–23), in

which the Queen Mother of the West visits Emperor Wu. To the sound of pipes and drums in the clouds, the Queen Mother descends with hundreds of immortals riding on dragons and tigers, unicorns and cranes. The Queen Mother, who appears to be aged thirty or so and is of heavenly beauty, prepares a celestial banquet for the Emperor; and when she departs, music sounds as before and the air is filled with a sweet odour. For Chinese Paradise is but purified mundaneness with refined gratification of all the senses and indefinite prolongation of youth and vigour.

In 'Yang Kung-cheng' also by Li Fu-yen, a powerful fragrance fills the air and, to the sound of music, a heavenly procession descends to the cottage of a village woman chosen to be an immortal, to escort her to Yün-t'ai Peak on the holy mountain, Hwa-shan, whither she proceeds, seated on a white crane, flanked by coloured clouds and preceded by ornamental spears and banners. Having been installed an immortal, she is allotted a place on the enchanted P'eng-lai Island (which also figures in our tale) but returns, as a filial daughter-in-law, to her cottage to care for her decrepit father-in-law during his lifetime (see General Introduction, p. 22, *supra*; *T'ai-p'ing kuang-chi*, c. 68, pp. 421 – 3).

P'eng-lai Island was one of three islands said to be in the sea off Shantung Province inhabited by immortals, where the elixir of life was to be had, the other two being Fang-chang and Ying-chou; rulers had been in quest of these enchanted islands since the fourth century B.C. (see *Shih chi*, c. 28, punctuated ed., pp. 1369 – 70; *Han shu*, c. 25a, punctuated ed., pp. 1204 – 5). Prince's House Mountain, situated not, in fact, in Yangchow Prefecture, but on the border between Shansi and Honan provinces, has immortal associations; it is listed, for instance, in *Pao-p'u-tzu nei-p'ien chiao-shih*, c. 4, p. 76, among the mountains that harbour immortals. Altar to Heaven Peak is its highest peak.

Yangchow (in Kiangsu Province), situated on the Grand Canal, was an important commercial centre and a cosmopolitan city in the T'ang, a place of fabulous wealth in which fortunes were made overnight, as is illustrated in the following anecdote :

> When some travellers met, they each told the others what they aimed at in life. One said that he would like to be Prefect of Yangchow; another that he would like to amass great wealth; still another that he would like to rise to heaven, mounted on a crane. One of them said, however, that he would like to have a hundred thousand strings of cash girded round his loins and fly on the back of a crane to Yangchow, thus combining the wishes of the three.
>
> (*Shang Yün hsiao-shuo*, p. 3a in *Shuo fu*, ed. of 1647, c. 46)

The dark-skinned slave also occurs in the tale 'The Blackamoor Slave' by P'ei Hsing (*T'ang-jen hsiao-shuo*, pp. 267–9).

In 'T'ao Hsien', a swarthy slave, an experienced sailor and diver, who was the gift to the hero from a Prefect on the south coast, is killed by a dragon in a river (see General Introduction, p. 18, *supra*; *T'ai-p'ing kuang-chi*, c. 420, pp. 3421–3).

'Old Chang' is in *T'ang-jen hsiao-shuo*, pp. 235–8, and *T'ai-p'ing kuang-chi*, c. 16, pp. 112–5. Its author was Li Fu-yen of the ninth century.

Old Chang

Old Chang was an aged market gardener in Liuho in Yangchow Prefecture (in Kiangsu Province). Among his neighbours was Wei Shu, who had served as a petty official in Yangchow in the middle (around 510) of the T'ien-chien reign of the Liang dynasty. When Wei summoned a matchmaker in the neighbourhood to find a husband for his eldest daughter, who had just attained maturity, Old Chang hearing about it, waited in high spirits outside Wei's gate, and when the matchmaker came out, insisted on inviting her to his house, where he plied her with food and wine. At the end of the meal, Old Chang said, 'I hear that the Weis have a daughter of marriageable age and that they are asking you to look for a husband for her. Is that correct?' The matchmaker confirming that it was, Old Chang continued: 'To be sure, I am not young; but I earn a decent living as a market gardener. Pray woo her for me, and if my suit prove successful, I shall reward you well'. But the matchmaker only gave Chang a good scolding. A few days later, Old Chang again inviting the matchmaker to his house, the woman said, 'Why do you not take a good look at yourself, old man? Would the daughter of an official's family marry an aged and decrepit market gardener? Of course they are not well off; but there are numerous officials' families who would desire such a match, whereas you certainly are far from eligible. If I spoke up for you merely because I had accepted your hospitality, I should really be insulted'. Old Chang persisted : 'All I ask is that you bring up my suit, which, in the event of its proving unacceptable, I shall only blame fate'. In spite of herself, therefore, the matchmaker took the liberty of advancing Old Chang's suit with the family.

Outraged by the effrontery of the proposal, Wei said in a fury, 'Is it because you think we are poor that you have come thus to affront us ? The Wei family would have no truck with that sort of person. Who does he think he is to come forward with such a suit ? Though a fool need not be answerable for his actions, you should have shown more sense in going about your business'. The matchmaker said in reply, 'It was not the kind of offer that I would usually have brought up, but the old man compelled me to speak for him'. Wei now said in a huff, 'Then bring him this reply : he has our consent if within the next few days he can provide five hundred strings of cash as a betrothal gift'. When the matchmaker came out and told Old Chang, he simply said, 'Very well', and before long had filled a cart with five hundred strings of cash and sent it to the Weis. The family were utterly amazed. Wei cried out, 'But that was spoken in jest! Besides, how should a market gardener come into all this money ? I said "five hundred strings" to put him off, and now he has brought this cartload of cash. What shall we do ?' And he sent a servant to watch his daughter in secret, but she seemed resigned to her fate. Wei thereupon saying, 'Perhaps all this was pre-ordained!', agreed to the match.

After marrying Miss Wei, Old Chang carried on as a market gardener. He dug the ground and minded the compost and sold his vegetables as before, and his wife did the cooking and the washing uncomplainingly. The sight of the pair of them toiling and moiling became an embarrassment to the Weis' relatives, but there was nothing that they could do. After a few years, one relative, wiser than the rest, openly reproved Wei, saying, 'To be sure, you were poor;

but there were many poor families in the district. Were you obliged to marry your daughter to an old and feeble market gardener? Since in effect you have disavowed her, why do you not ask them to go away?' Acting upon this advice, Wei prepared a dinner several days later for his daughter and Old Chang, and when all were merry with drink, dropped a hint. Old Chang immediately stood up and said, 'The reason we have not left this place until now is lingering sentiment. Since you are tired of us, we shall gladly depart. Under Prince's House Mountain I have a small farm and we return there tomorrow morning'. And before it was dawn he took his wife with him to bid the Weis farewell, saying, 'If in years to come you should think of your daughter, you could send the oldest brother to visit us in our home south of Altar to Heaven Peak'. Old Chang then made his wife put on her coolie hat and mount a donkey, while he himself followed with a stick in hand. And they were gone and not heard of again.

Several years later, Wei thought of his daughter, imagining her to be grimy and dishevelled, and ordered his son I-fang to visit his sister. I-fang coming across a blackamoor slave ploughing with an ox to the south of Altar to Heaven Peak, asked, 'Is there a farm of Old Chang's near by?' The slave said, leaving the plough and bowing down, 'Why have you been so long in coming, Master Eldest? The farm is quite near. I will lead the way'. And they headed for the east, at first ascending a hill, below which was a river, then crossing the river and on through a dozen or so landscapes which seemed quite out of this world, eventually descending a hill to come in view of a red-gated mansion with pavilions and turrets and a variety of flowers and trees to the north of a stream. Clouds and mists cast an airy tint over the scenery; while phoenixes and cranes and peacocks glided and fluttered over the grounds, and voices singing and the melodious sound of pipes filled the air. The blackamoor pointing to the mansion and saying, 'This is "Chang's Farm",' I-fang was startled beyond measure.

When he reached the gate, a servant in purple livery ushered him into the parlour, the furniture and hangings and ornaments of which were all so sumptuous as he had never seen before; and the room was pervaded by a rare scent, which seeped into the valley. The tinkle of jade pendants proclaimed the approach of two maids, who greeted I-fang, saying, 'So Master Eldest has arrived!' Then a dozen maids, all of exquisite beauty, came out in pairs, forming a procession preceding a man arrayed in a silk hat, red silk robes and red shoes, who emerged slowly from a door. One of the maids leading I-fang forward to bow to his host, who was of majestic appearance and whose countenance exuded youth and freshness, I-fang upon looking closely, saw that it was Old Chang, who saluted him by saying, 'Life is a burden. Man lives in a furnace; and before he has purified himself, the flame of new desires is kindled, so that there is not a moment of ease. How have you been amusing yourself in this wearisome journey that is life, brother-in-law? Your sister is at her toilet, and will see you presently'. And bowing, Old Chang asked I-fang to be seated.

Before long, a maid coming in, said, 'The mistress has finished combing her hair', and Old Chang led I-fang into the main hall, where brother and sister greeted each other. The beams in the hall were made of aloes-wood, the doors of tortoise shell, the windows of jade, the door-screens of pearls, and the steps of a cold, green substance which I-fang could not make out. As for his sister's attire, it was so ornate as was seldom seen among men. After exchanging civilities with I-fang, Old Chang and his wife asked after the health of older relatives, but somewhat insolently. Soon dinner was served, the viands consisting of the choicest dainties and delicacies, after which, I-fang was lodged in the inner parlour.

At dawn on the following day, while Old Chang was sitting with I-fang, a maid came up and whispered in the ear of her master, who said laughing, 'Since we have our visitor here, to return at dusk would be too late'. Then turning to

I-fang, he said, 'My sister is making a trip to P'eng-lai Island with your sister as companion; but as we shall be back before dusk, please rest here in the meantime'. And with a bow, he went within. Shortly afterwards, clouds gathered in the courtyard, while phoenixes hovered above, and stringed and wind instruments issued forth their trembling notes. Old Chang and his wife and sister each riding on the back of a phoenix and their dozen followers each on a crane, all rose in the air and headed due east, soon disappearing from view to the fading sound of music. I-fang, who stayed behind, was carefully waited on by a young maid. Before dusk, the party returned to the strains of reed-organs. Upon descending into the courtyard, Old Cheng and his wife greeted I-fang, saying, It must have been tedious, being alone all day. But this is the realm of the gods, where mortals are debarred. You have been admitted on account of your karma, though even you may not remain long. Tomorrow we shall send you off'.

On the morrow, I-fang's sister came out, asking him to convey messages of filial duty to their parents, and bidding him farewell, while Old Chang added: 'The mundane world is cut off from here and we shall not be writing'. And presenting I-fang with twenty gold ingots and an old straw hat, Old Chang said, 'If you are short of funds, you can go to the herbalist Old Wang in front of the Northern Palace of Yangchow and ask for ten thousand strings of cash, using the hat as a token', upon which they parted. The blackamoor slave having been ordered to accompany I-fang, went with him as far as Altar to Heaven Peak, where the slave bowed and took his leave, I-fang then returning home with the gold.

The Wei family were astonished to hear I-fang's account of his visit, some of them considering Old Chang to be a god and others, a wizard. After five or six years, when the gold had all been spent, they thought of obtaining from Old Wang the money vouched for, yet feared that Old Chang had simply made up a tall story. And some of them said, 'For such a sum, how could there have been no written acknowledgement, only

a straw hat to serve as token?' But then, finding themselves
in straits, the family made I-fang go, saying, 'There is no
harm in trying, even if you get nothing'. So I-fang went to
Yangchow, where he found Old Wang laying out his medicine
at his stall outside the Northern Palace. Addressing Old
Wang, I-fang asked, 'What is your name, sir?' When Old
Wang gave his name, I-fang said, 'Old Chang asked me to
claim from you ten thousand strings of cash, with this hat as
a token.' Old Wang said, 'Although the money is there, I
cannot tell if the hat be really his'. Upon I-fang saying, 'You
can examine it. Do you not know it?', before Old Wang
could speak, his daughter came out from behind a cloth
curtain and said, 'Old Chang came on one occasion to ask me
to patch up the crown of his hat, and since I had no black
thread at the time, I used a red one. I can check the thread
and the stitching'. And upon examining the thread, she said
it was indeed the same hat. I-fang then returning home
loaded with the money, they all believed that Old Chang was
a god.

The family again missing their daughter, sent I-fang once
more to look for his sister southwards of Altar to Heaven
Peak. When he got there, the terrain had altered: there were
scores of hills and rivers, but not any roads. Meeting some
woodcutters, I-fang inquired of them, but none had heard of
Old Chang's farm. I-fang returning, filled with melancholy
thoughts, the family concluded that there could be no further
contact between the mundane world and the gods. Then they
looked for Old Wang, who had also disappeared. A few years
later, I-fang happening to be before the Northern Palace in
Yangchow, saw the blackamoor slave of the Changs approach,
saying, 'How is the family, Master Eldest? Although my
mistress may not return home, she is informed on all that
goes on in the house, as if she herself were present'. And
taking out ten catties of gold from his bosom, he presented it
to I-fang, saying, 'My mistress bids me give you this',
adding: 'My master and Old Wang are drinking in this

wine shop. Pray sit and wait, while I go in to announce you'. And I-fang sat under the wine-seller's flag until dusk, and never saw any of them come out; he then went into the shop to see for himself, but although the place was full of customers, neither Old Chang nor Old Wang was there, nor was the blackamoor slave. But the gold was real, and I-fang returned, overwhelmed with wonder. And the gold lasted several more years, though there was no further news of Old Chang.

'Wang Hsieh or Dark Robe Land'

There exist two versions of this tale, a brief one containing a mere skeleton of the plot and the poems exchanged between the hero and the heroine, who is the Princess of the strange island, and the more elaborate one here translated. Both versions appear in collections with which the Sung story-writer and editor Liu Fu, who lived in the eleventh century, was connected (see 'Introduction' to *Ch'ing-so kao-i*, Ku-tien 1958, pp. 1–2; the brief version is quoted in *Ku-chin t'u-shu chi-ch'eng*, xix 25, 'Swallows', 'Additional Matter', p. 3a). The longer one is a reworking, probably by Liu Fu himself, of the brief version.

In this tale, which is the only example in this volume from the Sung, the verse approximates to colloquial speech. As far as the supernatural is concerned, a new departure seems to be the attempt to reveal the heroine's true identity through her description: 'On the wedding day, Hsieh took a close look at his bride, finding her to have bright eyes and a slender waist, an apricot-shaped face and purple temples; and withal so light and graceful that she seemed to glide on air . . .'

The locality of the tale is significant. It is a Nanking story, in which the name of the hero, Wang Hsieh, is the combination of the names of the two leading families in the Southern Capital in the fourth, fifth and sixth centuries, the

Wang and the Hsieh, who had their official residences in Dark Robe Lane, frequented even then by swallows (see Volume II 'Nature Poetry' of this series, pp. 40–1). Outside Nanking, overlooking the Yangtze river, is the famous Swallows' Rock, a spot at which until recently tens of thousands of swallows fluttered in the spring and summer months, flying just a few inches above people's heads. And the quotation from the T'ang poet Liu Yü-hsi (772–842) at the end of the tale should read:

> The swallows that once haunted the halls of the Wang and the Hsieh
>
> May now be seen on the beams of ordinary dwellings.

The poem is in *Liu Pin-k'o wen-chi*, Ssu-pu pei-yao ed., c. 24, pp. 3b–4a.

By 'Mei Ch'eng of the Han dynasty', who is referred to in the King's speech, is probably intended Mei Fu, the Han hermit who, according to legend, spent some time on the island of Puto-shan off the coast of Chekiang Province. From this association, Puto-shan is also known as 'Mei-ch'en' (Mei's Peak'). Thus 'Mei Ch'eng, the name occurring in our tale, is probably a corruption of 'Mei Fu'.

In 'Anecdotes from the K'ai-yüan and T'ien-pao reigns of the T'ang' by Wang Jen-yü (tenth century) there is also a tale about a swallow that carries on its leg a poem from a wife left behind in the capital Ch'ang-an to her husband engaged in commerce in Hunan (*K'ai-yüan T'ien-pao i-shih*, pp. 9b–10b, in *Ku-shih wen-fang hsiao-shuo*, Commercial Press 1925).

'Wang Hsieh' is in Lu Hsün (ed.), *T'ang Sung ch'uan-ch'i chi*, Ku-tien 1955, pp. 302–7, and *Ch'ing-so kao-i*, pp. 207–11.

Wang Hsieh or Dark Robe Land

Wang Hsieh of the T'ang dynasty, who was very rich, was from a family in Chin-ling (i.e. Nanking) who had for generations been engaged in sailing the seas. One day, Hsieh had a ship fitted out and set out on a voyage to Arabia. After sailing for over a month, a gale rising and the sea raging, the sky was covered by ink-coloured clouds and the billows were like mountains. Whales and huge sea-turtles came and went, and hordes of all kinds of fish, agitating the waves. The winds ever increasing in force, the crest of the waves raised the ship as high as the skies, and when they had gone east, it plunged as if to the very depths of the ocean, with all on board swaying and rolling with the vessel. Soon the ship was wrecked, Hsieh alone clinging to a plank and drifting with the wind and the waves. Looking about him, he could see strange fish and sea animals to his left and right, their mouths wide open in readiness, to devour him. So he kept his eyes shut, expecting to perish at any moment.

After three days, Hsieh was cast ashore on an island, and abandoning his plank, walked on dry land. When he had gone for a hundred or so paces, he met an old couple, aged over seventy, both clad in black, who greeted him gleefully, addressing him as their master and asking why he had travelled there. Upon Hsieh telling them what had happened, they led him to their house, and, when Hsieh was seated, said, 'Our master has come a long way; he must be famished'. And they brought him food, which was but fish and marine delicacies. After over a month, when Hsieh had recovered from his journey and was eating and drinking normally, the old man said, 'All who visit our country must meet our King. At the beginning I thought you were tired and not in a fit state for an audience. Now you are ready'. To which Hsieh agreed. The old man now leading the way, they walked for three *li*, passing the market and dwelling houses and throngs of inhabitants, and after crossing a long bridge, saw the palace with its succession of terraces and pavilions, like the dwelling of a prince or nobleman in Hsieh's own country.

When they reached the main gate, a porter went in to announce them, and before long, an elegantly dressed woman came out and said, 'The King summons the gentleman to an audience'. Seated in the audience hall with a row of women standing on either side, the King, who wore a black robe and a black hat, said, when Hsieh reached the steps leading into the hall, 'Our etiquette does not apply to you, who are from the northern sphere, and you need not bow'. Hsieh said, 'Since I have come to your country, it is only right that I bow down before the King'. Hsieh then bowing, the King half-bowed in return; and being pleased, the King bade Hsieh enter the hall and be seated. The King asked, 'How did you, worthy sir, come to visit our remote country?' Hsieh replied, 'I was shipwrecked in a storm on the high seas and came hither by chance. I beg for the King's mercy'. The King then asking, 'Where are you staying?', Hsieh replied that he was lodged in the house of his host. The King at once summoning Hsieh's host, the old man came forward and reported thus to the King: 'In his own country our visitor was my master, and I have endeavoured to please him in all things'. Then saying, 'You may report to us, if he should require anything', the King dismissed them, and the old man led Hsieh back to the house.

The old couple had a daughter, who was very beautiful and who sometimes brought the tea; at other times, Hsieh would peep at her through the curtains, and she did not seem to mind his attentions. One day, being invited by the old man to drink with him, Hsieh, when half tipsy, said, 'I have been living in a strange country and owe my preservation to yourself and your good lady. Though I am here but as a traveller, your great kindness has made me feel at home. Nevertheless, I am quite alone in your world, single and pitiable, and being prone to depression, can neither sleep soundly nor take delight in my food. I much fear that this might lead to illness and cause me to become a burden to you'. The old man then said, 'I have been meaning to speak to you, prevented only by the fear of giving offence. I have a daughter aged seventeen, who was born in my master's home. It is my wish to marry her to you, so that she might comfort you in your sojourn here. What do you think of my proposal?' Upon which Hsieh cried, 'Excellent!' The old man then chose an auspicious day and prepared the gifts, with the King also conferring gifts of wine and food to express approbation of the alliance. On the wedding day, Hsieh took a close look at his bride, finding her to have bright eyes and a slender waist, an apricot-shaped face and purple temples, and withal so light and graceful that she seemed to glide on air; she was indeed most bewitching in appearance.

When Hsieh asked her the name of the country, she replied, 'Dark Robe Land'. Hsieh then said, 'Your father would often refer to me as his master; but I never knew him until I came here and certainly never employed him. How, then, could I be his master?' And she replied, 'You will know in the course of time'. Later on, in the midst of feasting and drinking, or at bed time, she would often become shy and apprehensive, shedding tears with her eyebrows closely knit. When Hsieh asked her why she wept, she said, 'I fear that before long we shall part'. Hsieh would then say, 'Although

H

I am in a foreign country, you have made me forget to return.
Why do you speak of parting?' And his bride would say,
'It is decreed by fate and beyond our help'.

Then the King invited Hsieh to a banquet in Precious Ink
Hall, in which all the furnishings and all the utensils were
black, as well as the instruments of the musicians, who played
airy and pleasing tunes which he had never heard before,
while the cups flowed with wine. The King then ordering
that black jade cups be brought, said, turning to Hsieh,
'Only two men have ever come from your country to ours.
There was Mei Ch'eng of the Han dynasty, and now there
is yourself. We would wish you to leave a composition for
us to form part of the lore of our land in the future'. Pen and
paper being then brought at the King's command, Hsieh
made a poem:

> Following the family tradition, I loaded my ship,
> Accustomed to sail ten thousand *li* on the seas.
> This year, alas, luck was against me,
> My journey ending unexpectedly in disaster.

> The gale raged like a pursuing army
> With, for banners, layer upon layer of dark-coloured
>   clouds,
> And fishes and sea animals in battle array:
> The crew were all buried in a watery grave.

> The lightning flashed its purple flames overhead;
> The angry billows lashed against the horizon.
> The whale's blood-shot eyes turned the sea red;
> The sea-turtles stirred up high the white foam.

> The mast broke and fell, dividing the ocean,
> In a thunderous clash that sealed the ship's fate.
> Helped by the gods, I alone did not sink,
> But clung to a plank and reached this shore.

> The King is most gracious to invite him to a feast,
> But the traveller remains disconsolate,
> His gaze turned homewards, his tears flowing:
> Oh that he could sprout a pair of wings!

The King read the lines with pleasure and said, 'Your poem is very good. You need not long for home, for we shall soon send you back, and even though you have no wings, we shall cause you to fly through the air'. When, after returning from the banquet, [Hsieh showed his wife the poem],* she said, 'How you do mock us in your last line!', a remark which Hsieh failed to understand.

Before long, the sea being calm, the breezes gentle, and the days warm, Hsieh's wife said, weeping, 'You will soon be gone!' And the King sent a messenger to tell Hsieh that a day had been chosen on which he was to return home, and asking him to bid members of his family farewell. His wife then prepared a parting feast, although she was weeping so much that she could not speak, her cheeks being stained by tears spilling all over her, her countenance sorrowful, and her body emaciated. Hsieh, too, was filled with sorrow. And Hsieh's wife wrote a parting poem:

> Our union is all too brief and transient:
> Of old, conjugal ties were not always binding.
> Alone behind a curtain I shall lament at night
> With my soul borne northwards by the gentle winds.

And she said, 'From now on, I shall not go north. For you must not see me other than as I am, or you might loathe, and forswear your love for, me; and I should be jealous if I saw you surrounded by your family. I shall, therefore, no longer migrate to the north, but will end my days here in my home land. Nor must you bring anything from here—though not because of their value—save only this—'. And she ordered a servant to fetch an elixir-pill, saying, 'This pill enables one to summon back the soul of anyone who has been dead for

* I have emended the sentence, the original being obscure.

less than a month, if used according to these directions. First, place a mirror on the chest of the dead person and then the pill on the nape of the neck. Next, cauterize with moxa, which will instantly bring about the revival of the dead person. It is vigilantly guarded by the gods of the main, and can cross the sea only if kept in a box made of K'un-lun jade'. A jade box being then found, they put the pill in it and tied it to Hsieh's left arm, after which husband and wife parted in the utmost grief.

The King then said to Hsieh, 'Our land yields nothing with which we can be proud to present you'. And calling for paper, the King wrote a poem:

> While on a journey to the Southern Ocean,
> Adrift you chanced upon our land.
> From now on we shall no longer meet,
> Separated by ten thousand *li* of clouds and water.

Hsieh bowing to bid the King farewell, the King ordered that the flying sedan be brought, which was a sedan-chair covered with black felt. When Hsieh had seated himself in it, water was fetched from the Pond of Wings and sprinkled on the sedan. The King then sent for Hsieh's host and his wife, directing them to escort Hsieh home, finally saying to Hsieh, 'Shut your eyes and you will reach your home after a little while; but if you opened your eyes, you would drop into the ocean'. With his eyes shut, Hsieh heard the winds and waves roaring, and after a long time, opening his eyes again, found himself sitting in the hall of his house with no one near him except two swallows twittering on the beam. With his eyes fixed on them in an upward glance, Hsieh realized that he had been in the Kingdom of the Swallows.

Soon afterwards, members of Hsieh's household came out to ask how he was, saying, 'We heard that your ship had been wrecked and thought you were dead. How were you able to return?' Hsieh said, 'I alone stayed afloat clutching a plank', but kept silent about his sojourn in Dark Robe Land.

At the time Hsieh left home, he had a son who was then three years old; not seeing the boy, Hsieh asked about him and learnt that his son had died a fortnight before, whereupon he burst into tears. But suddenly remembering the pill, he ordered that the boy be taken out of the coffin and cauterized in the way he had been instructed, and the boy indeed revived.

By autumn the swallows on the beam, on the point of departure for the south, twittered mournfully in the hall, and when Hsieh beckoned to them, they alighted on his arm. Hsieh then wrote a poem on a tiny sheet of paper, which he tied to the tail of one of the swallows:

> Mischance brought me to your enchanted island,
> Where I won your pity and your love.
> Excluded from your presence with my flight home,
> At each thought of you I still weep anew.

In the spring, the two swallows returning, made directly for Hsieh's arm, and a note tied to the tail of one of them contained a poem:

> When we met, it was a case of predestination;
> When we parted, the grief was all too real.
> In the spring you receive a poem,
> But your swallow-mate remains absent.

Hsieh was filled with deep regret, and the following year the swallows no longer came. Later, Hsieh's adventure became known and was much talked about, so that the street in which he dwelt came to be called Dark Robe Lane. Liu Yü-hsi in his 'Five Poems on Nanking' has one entitled 'Dark Robe Lane':

> By Scarlet Bird Bridge the wild flowers bloom
>   in profusion;
> Upon Dark Robe Lane the setting sun casts its rays.
> The swallows that once haunted the ornate hall of
>   Wang Hsieh
> May now be seen on the beams of ordinary dwellings,

which proves that the tale is well-founded.

Liao-chai chih-i

Liao-chai chih-i

Chinese literature about the supernatural realm was vastly enriched in the seventeenth century by a collection of tales in classical prose by P'u Sung-ling (1640–1715). The collection, *Liao-chai chih-i*, first completed in 1679 but with later additions and revisions, circulated in manuscript for many decades before it was printed in the next century, long after the author's death, the earliest extant edition being that of 1766. Its author led an uneventful life in his native county of Tzechwan in Shantung Province, passing his licentiate's examination early but having no success in the higher examinations. A spell as private secretary to the Magistrate Sun Hui took him at the age of thirty-one to Paoying and Kaoyu and Yangchow in Kiangsu Province. And from the time he was forty until he was seventy, he served as tutor in the local Pi family. He seems to have cherished great ambitions, for apart from his literary compositions, he busied himself in writing imaginary laudatory memorials submitted by high officials to the throne. But P'u did not lead a completely obscure existence, and included among his literary friends the celebrated poet and critic Wang Shih-chen (1634–1711), who wrote comments on a number of P'u's stories, and the poet and critic Chang Tu-ch'ing, who was from P'u's county.

P'u's father, although from a family of scholars, had for

some time also been a merchant, and in P'u's tales, commercial astuteness is extolled rather than despised. And P'u
was fortunate in his marriage. At the age of thirteen, his
wife, a Miss Liu, was sent ahead of time to the P'u family
because of rumours of a search being made in the region for
ladies for service in the Palace, and slept in the same bed as
her mother-in-law, the wedding taking place two years later,
when P'u was eighteen. Soon afterwards, the family property
was divided up; the main buildings having been allotted to the
other brothers, P'u received, as his share, three dilapidated
rooms round a courtyard overgrown with weeds on the
family farm. With a white board P'u and his wife devised a
makeshift partition in their principal room to preserve some
privacy. Miss Liu proved a model wife, indifferent to her
husband's worldly fortunes, and it was her frugality and
sound management of the household that ensured that in
their old age, surrounded by children and grandchildren,
they were not entirely destitute.

Such then was the author's situation: decent poverty
amidst drab surroundings, unrecognised talent underlined by
periodic examination failures, frustration relieved only by
day-dreaming. Such, too, is the situation in which so many
of the heroes in his tales find themselves. But P'u also took a
consuming interest in the supernatural, as he himself declares
in his Preface to his collection of tales, penned in 1679:

> Though without the gifts of the erudite Kan Pao,[1] I
> have long sought immortal lore; and like the hospitable
> Su Tung-p'o, I love to hear all and sundry discourse on
> ghosts. Having heard their accounts, I put pen to paper,
> and so the tales have piled up. In time, friends from all
> over the land begin to send me reports by post . . . (p.1)

Interest was strengthened by belief in reincarnation. He
himself, he conjectured, had been a Buddhist monk in a
previous existence:

> At the time of my birth, my late father dreamt about a
> thin and sickly monk entering the room, with his right

> shoulder bare and a poultice the size of a cash coin on his
> right breast. I was born with a patch on my breast at the
> same spot when my father woke up. What was more,
> when I was young, I was thin and often ill, and seemed
> to be without hopes of a long life. Our house was as
> desolate and cold as a monk's cell, and my livelihood,
> that of ploughing with my pen, as unrewarding as a
> monk's begging bowl. Scratching my head, I often
> wondered : Could it be that I was indeed a mendicant
> friar in my last existence ? (p. 2)

As for the tales :

> I stitched the bits and pieces together into a garment
> and claim to have written a sequel to Liu I-ching's 'In
> the World of the Shades';[2] but my clumsy endeavours,
> heated by drink, have only resulted in a work that gives
> vent to my private grief and indignation (p. 3).

The resulting work does indeed contain much satire and
unconcealed criticism, chiefly of bureaucracy and officialdom,
and of examiners and the examination system. The workings
of bureaucracy extend to heaven and hell. In 'The Goddess'
(c.10), a deity of the underworld having given offence to a
colleague, requires the intercession of the local mundane
governor in the form of a document complete with official
seal, at his arraignment before the Emperor of Heaven
(p.1317). In 'Hsi Fang-p'ing' (c.10), the hero fights
injustice in court after court in the nether regions :

> And Hsi reflected that the corruption and injustice in hell
> was even worse than that in the world of men (p.1343).

In 'Liu Ch'üan' (c.12), an official position in the underworld
may be purchased (pp.1651–2). 'Bureau of Investigation into
Abuse and Corruption' (c.6) is a savage exposure of double-
faced officialdom, supposedly in hell (pp. 822–5). And in
'Chang A-tuan' (c.5), the process of reincarnation may be
arrested through bribery of the clerk concerned (p. 629).

As for examinations, they, too, are held in the underworld
for recruitment to the infernal civil service. In 'Yü Ch'ü-o'

(c.9), a ghost candidate for an examination in hell is in the habit of burning model essays and swallowing their ashes so as to fill his insides with them. He is eventually set this subject: 'The eighteen layers of hell have insufficient room for the ever growing number of offenders. Discuss in detail all possible means of dealing with the increasingly numerous and wicked culprits' (p.1168). And in 'Three Reincarnations' (c.10), unsuccessful candidates demand that Yama pluck out an incompetent examiner's eyes for having been blind to merit; and the feud between their leader and the unfortunate examiner lasts through several reincarnations (pp. 1330–2).

But most of the tales have as their theme the fantasy of fulfilment, frequently brought about through supernatural agents, especially fox spirits and disembodied souls. In a few tales, the settings in which these supernatural beings appear make us immediately aware of their divinity. In 'P'ien-p'ien' (c.3), the prodigal son Lo Tzu-fu, who has lost his way at dusk, is invited by the goddess P'ien-p'ien to stay in her cave:

> Overjoyed, he followed her deep into the mountains, when they saw a grotto. Entering, he found, near the opening, a flowing stream with a stone bridge over it; a few steps forward brought them to two stone chambers, illumined as by daylight, so that there was no need of lantern or candle. (pp. 432–3)

In 'Princess of the West Lake' (c.5), Ch'en Pi-chiao chances upon the hunting party of the daughter of the Dragon King of Tungting Lake on a hill, and, so as to keep out of their sight, hurriedly makes his way down:

> Half-hidden among the thick woods were halls and towers. Thinking it was a monastery, he drew near and found a white-washed surrounding wall beside a splashing stream, and a stone bridge leading to a red gate, which was half open. Peering through the gate, he saw pavilions and terraces as in an Imperial park or the estate of some nobleman. Ch'en made his way in through rambling creepers and fragrant blossoms, and

after passing several winding galleries, came upon
another garden court, in which scores of weeping
willows reached up to the red eaves of the wings of the
house and flower petals glided through the air to the
cawing pheasants, while elm leaves fell, borne by gentle
breezes. It was indeed a most delightful scene, out of
this world. And crossing a pavilion, he saw a high
swing . . . (p. 647)

And the home of Ying-ning (c. 2), daughter of a fox
mother, is full of enchantment as it appears to the hero,
Wang Tzu-fu:

After walking for thirty *li* or so, he found himself among
layer upon layer of mountains, surrounded by bracing
and invigorating blue-green haze. The winding paths
being quite deserted, he looked down into the valley
and saw, hidden amidst the thick clusters of flowering
trees, a hamlet, and descended towards it. He came into
view of a few thatched cottages, neat and elegant in
appearance, and also a house facing north, with weeping
willows before the gate and peach and apricot trees
mingling with tall bamboos behind the wall, and birds
singing among the trees. For fear of intruding into a
private garden, he sat down to rest on a clean, smooth
slab of stone opposite (p. 149).

Or, under the moon or the flame of the candle, lovelorn
scholars in their solitary rooms are visited by amorous
female ghosts or fox spirits, as in 'Hung-yü' (c. 2, p. 276),
'Lien-suo' (c. 3, pp. 331–2), 'Hu Ssu-chieh' (c. 2, p. 201) and
'Liu Ssu-niang' (c. 2, p. 286). In 'Hsiao-hsieh' (c. 6), the
pure-hearted T'ao Wang-san acquires under such conditions
two ghostly lady pupils (pp. 772–5). In 'Chang A-tuan'
(c. 5), the female ghost, out of selfless devotion to the hero,
conjures up the spirit of his dead wife (pp. 627–9). And in
'A Dream of Foxes' (c. 5), on account of his interest in foxes,
Pi I-an, the author's friend and faithful reader, is visited by
a fox mother and her daughter, who, after over a year's

association with Pi, asks that her story be also included in
Liao-chai chih-i (pp. 618–22). Or the transformation may
occur under the hero's very eyes. In 'The Student from
Eastern Chekiang' (c. 12), a fox falls on the hero's bed and
is later transformed into a beautiful woman (p. 1701). And
in 'Dog Lamp' (c. 3), a lamp falling out of an upstairs
window turns into a dog and then a woman (p. 406).

But there usually are human complications, and the plot
moves between the supernatural and the human plane. The
tale of 'Hung-yü' is typical. Feng Hsiang-ju, a poor graduate
who has lost, first, his mother and, then, his wife, and lives
with his father in Kwangping (in Hopeh Province) is visited
on a moonlit night by an attractive woman 'from next door'
calling herself Hung-yü. Their clandestine meetings continue
for half a year, when they are discovered by Feng's father,
who reproves them both for their misconduct. Thereupon
Hung-yü terminates her visits after advising Feng to marry
a Miss Wei of another village and providing him with forty
ounces of silver as a betrothal gift. Miss Wei turns out to be
both beautiful and virtuous, and after two years, gives birth
to a son. While on her way home after sweeping the tombs
of the ancestors, she is noticed by the lecherous former
Censor Sung, who dispatches a servant to induce Feng to
part with his wife, offering a large sum of money in com-
pensation. Feng and his father being both outraged, Feng's
father reviles the servant in no uncertain terms. Sung then
orders his men to beat up father and son, and to abduct the
wife, Feng's father dying as a result of his injuries, while
Feng's wife makes away with herself in captivity. After
filing a suit against Sung to no avail, Feng in his despair is
visited by a stranger, who offers to avenge him; thereupon
Feng flees with his infant son into the hills, and that night
Sung and his two sons are murdered. Feng is apprehended
and abandons his infant son in a valley, but is eventually set
free and returns to his home, heart-broken. Presently, a
knock is heard and in walks Hung-yü, who turns out to be,

not the woman 'from next door', but a fox. She has rescued his son, whom she now produces. At once, too, she sets about the task of housekeeping, buying looms and hiring farm labourers :

> And in the ensuing examination he obtained his second degree. He was then thirty-six. And his fields continued to increase in extent and his house soon became a mansion. And Hung-yü, who seemed so delicate that she would flutter in the wind, worked harder than a peasant woman, not sparing herself even in the depth of winter, though her hands remained as soft as lard. And though she claimed to be thirty-eight, she looked twenty . . . (p. 282)

Examination success, female society leading to domestic bliss, prospering descendants and an abundance of worldly goods : these circumscribe the horizon of our author. P'u's own attitude towards the marvellous events he recounts oscillates between credulity and make-believe; by temperament, therefore, he was fitted for the task of continuing the tradition, as in his Preface he claims to set out to do, of Kan Pao and Liu I-ch'ing, and with his insatiable interest in ghosts and spirits, in death and revival, and in hell and reincarnation, he shows perhaps the greatest affinity to them and their fellow writers. But P'u also knew the T'ang *Ch'uan-ch'i* writers, and in *Liao-chai chih-i*, the pale and shadowy narrative of the early supernatural tale takes on the colours and flesh of the T'ang *ch'uan-ch'i* tale. That P'u has learnt his craft from the T'ang writers is clear from specific instances of imitation of T'ang tales.

In 'The General of Prodigious Strength' (c. 6), the general making an inventory of his possessions and offering half of his goods, servants and slave girls to his former benefactor (pp. 759–60) would seem to be based on the episode of the curly-bearded stranger relinquishing his property in favour of Li Ching in Tu Kuang-t'ing's 'Ch'iu-jan k'o' (*T'ang-jen hsiao-shuo*, pp. 180–1). In 'Chia Feng-chih' (c. 10), the hero

undergoing his trials in the mountain cave as one in quest of
the true way being misled by an apparition of his wife
(pp.1362–3) is reminiscent of Tu Tzu-ch'un undergoing
somewhat more arduous trials (Li Fu-yen, 'Tu Tzu-ch'un',
T'ang-jen hsiao-shuo, pp. 232–4). The tale, 'A Dream
World', is not only indebted to the two T'ang tales about
dreams, Shen Chi-chi's 'The Pillow' (*T'ang-jen hsiao-shuo*,
pp. 37–9) and Li Kung-tso's 'The Prefect of Nan-k'o'
(*T'ang-jen hsiao-shuo*, pp. 85–90), but also to 'Tu Tzu-ch'un'
for the hero Tseng's imaginary ordeal in undergoing the
tortures of hell and his subsequent reincarnation as a woman
(c. 4, pp. 518–27, esp. pp. 523–6). 'The Lotus Princess' (c. 5,
pp. 673–7), a tale about a swarm of bees, is transparently
based on 'The Prefect of Nan-h'o', a tale about an ant
kingdom. The tale, 'The Student from Feng-yang' (c. 2,
pp.187–9), in which three people have the same dream, is
probably based on Po Hsing-chien's 'Three Dreams'
(*T'ang-jen hsiao-shuo*, pp.108–9). In 'The Thunderer' (c. 3,
pp. 414–8), the hero taking part in rain-making and spilling
a larger share than customary over his native village is
probably indebted to Li Fu-yen's 'Rain-making' (see, *supra*,
pp. 79–83).

In resurrecting ghosts of historical figures, which he
delineates with considerable animation, P'u continues a
tradition of the Sung and Ming tales. In 'Marquis Huan'
(c.12), the ghost of Chang Fei, the general of the Three
Kingdoms period, reveals the golden touch to a traveller in
exchange for his horse (pp.1672–4). In 'Nieh Cheng' (c. 6),
the ghost of the faithful assassin of the Chou dynasty comes
out of his tomb to protect a woman from being abducted
(pp. 844–6). And 'Empress Chen' (c. 7) is about a brief
encounter between the Empress and a reincarnation of the
writer Liu Chen at her court (pp. 981–4). And in descending
to the level of the daily life of ordinary folk—and indeed
most of P'u's tales are about relatively humble men and
women—he follows in the steps of the Ming writers. In

'Wang Eldest' (c.11), a tale about gamblers, the humdrum experiences of villagers are interwoven into infernal paraphernalia (pp.1534–8). And in 'Yama' (c.5), the criminal act of a vicious woman in her family is projected in a scene in hell (pp.658–60). In theme and outlook, such tales show similarity to those of the Ming.

In narrative skill P'u transcends even his T'ang models. Not only does he create greater verisimilitude, but he endows his ostensibly supernatural characters with a liveliness or pathos only too human. The fox Hsiao-ts'ui, who confounds the machinations of her father-in-law's enemy at court through her romping and play-acting and who transforms her idiot boy-husband into a normal youth, is the very picture of a tomboy (c.7, pp.1000–8).

Hsiao-hsieh and Ch'iu-yung, the two ghost pupils of T'ao Wang-san, rival each other in schoolgirl mischief as in feminine assiduity (c.6, pp.772–9). The forever giggling Ying-ming, who cheers everyone up with her mirth, laughs so much that she is hardly able to complete her wedding ceremony (c.2, pp. 151–6). The ghost heroine in 'Huan-niang' (c.7) is so charmed by Wen Ju-ch'un playing on his guitar that she contrives a most desirable match for him merely for the privilege of hearing him play and being allowed herself to play on his instrument (pp.986–90). Even P'u's caricatures are at times moving, as in the lovesick Sun Tzu-ch'u, who chops off his extra finger in the hope of gaining the hand of A-pao and whose spirit flies to her bedchamber in the shape of a parrot (c.2, pp.233–6), or the bookworm Lang Yü-chu, who hunts among old books for a mate 'of jade-like beauty' (c.11, pp.1454–7).

The ghost lore in P'u's tales veers between the fantastic and the whimsical. Ghosts may return to live among men, marry and bear children. In 'Wan-hsia' (c.11), the ghost dancing couple, A-tuan and Wan-hsia, return to his family in Chinkiang (in Kiangsu Province) and a child is born to them, but the ineffably graceful Wan-hsia casts no shadow and,

I

with this as proof of her phantom nature, rejects the advances of the Prince, their patron (pp. 1476–81). Similarly, in 'The Poisonous Plant' (c. 2), a ghost son and daughter-in-law return to the family and remain with them until summoned to a higher calling among the gods (pp. 180–4). In 'The Ninth Miss Kung-sun' (c. 4), the hero enters the world of the dead and marries a ghost bride, who does not join him when he returns to the world of the living (pp. 477–83). And in 'Magistrate Lu's Daughter' (c. 3), the romance between the hero and ghost heroine continues in the heroine's next existence, with the hero rejuvenated so as to make a suitable bridegroom for the reborn ghost heroine (pp. 294–8).

Family relationships continue unchanged in the world of the dead. In 'Hsiang-ch'ün' (c. 10), the hero's ghost brother takes a ghost concubine, who gives birth to two ghost sons, one of whom is brought back to live in Yenan (in Shensi Province) with the hero, who also marries the ghost sister of the ghost brother's ghost concubine, the ghost bride being first subjected to a blood test and declared fit, since she bleeds when her arm is pricked by a needle, to marry a living person. In the same tale, the ghost bride Hsiang-ch'ün, at her husband's insistence, conjures up a beautiful woman ghost, who thereafter haunts the hero until the ghost brother intervenes (pp. 1322–9).

The tale of 'Ai-nu' (c. 9) begins with a ghost mother inviting a living tutor to teach her ghost son in a tomb on the road between Enhsien (in Shantung Province) and Hokien (in Hopeh Province). The tutor falls in love with the ghost maid-servant, Ai-nu, who eventually leaves with him, though remaining invisible to all except himself. Later, the tutor exhumes her corpse, and the ghost re-entering it, the ghost-corpse leads a half animate existence until one day he pours wine down its throat, whereupon it collapses (and the ghost, too, vanishes) (pp. 1191–5). In 'The Student Ch'u' (c. 8), a ghost student enters the body of a fellow student to pass an examination for him; then the ghost is reborn as the son of their tutor Lü, with the ghost's original surname Ch'u imprinted on the baby's palms (pp.1081–5). In 'Madam Liu' (c.9), a ghost grandmother supplies funds for a prospective grandson-in-law to go on a trading expedition and also furnishes him with a ghost horse, which disintegrates into dust and ashes many years later (pp.1289–95). In 'Wu Ch'iu-yüeh' (c.5), the hero kills, on two separate occasions, four ghost runners in order to lead his brother and the heroine back to life (pp.668–72). In 'The Drunkard' (c.4), a drunkard gets drunk in hell (pp.582–7) and in 'The Chess Fiend' (c.4), a chess addict remains incorrigible even after becoming a ghost (pp.532–3).

In *Liao-chai chih-i*, ghost lore is enmeshed in fox lore. As in earlier supernatural tales, fox spirits are sometimes visible, sometimes invisible. When visible, the female fox spirit is almost invariably beautiful, except in 'The Ugly Fox' (c.8), in which the fox has constantly to bribe her lover with gifts (pp.1107–9). In 'The Witty Fox' (c.4), the fox spirit takes part in the conversation but is invisible to all except the hero (pp.500–4). In 'Hu Fourth' (c.4), the fox friend reveals himself to the hero only at their moment of parting (pp.559–63). In 'The Student Kuo' (c.5), a fox spirit corrects a student's essays but never appears to him (pp.696–7). In 'But One Official' (c.12), only the voice of the fox spirit may be heard (pp.1704–5).

The author gives an account of his own experience of an actual session with a fox spirit in the third month of *Kuei-hai* year (1683) in 'The Fox Spirit' (c.5). At the house of the Liang family in Chi-hsia (near Lintze, about 45 kilometres from P'u's home in Tzechwan), a shrine was set up behind a red curtain, with a picture of the Bodhisatva Kuan-yin and some other pictures hanging on the wall, the altar consisting of a table with a small throne, a foot or so in height, on it. After offering incense, P'u and his friends heard the lady of the house sound the bell three times and mutter a prayer. The visitors being then told to sit and wait outside the curtain, the woman herself stood before it and talked to them about miracles wrought by the fox spirit. When, after some time, the visitors grew impatient, they asked the woman to invoke the spirit again. Sounds were then heard from behind the curtain, initially like the flapping of a bat, then like the crashing of a large stone on the altar, then like the sighing of an old man. The woman now going up to the throne, held a palm-leaf fan to conceal it, whereupon a loud voice was heard from behind the fan, saying, 'Surely our meeting was pre-ordained, gentlemen!' and continuing : 'What wise counsel have you to offer me?', whereupon some questions relating to Kuan-yin and Yama were asked, producing laconic answers, before someone made a request for medicine for a sick friend. At last, all their queries having been resolved, the visitors took their leave (pp. 691 – 2).

Fox lovers are sometimes injurious to the health of the beloved and sometimes harmless. In 'The Merchant's Son' (c. 1), the merchant's wife, haunted by a fox spirit, eventually dies, after her son has contrived to poison the fox (pp. 125 – 9). In 'Huang Ninth' (c. 3), a seductive male fox brings about the death of two male lovers, one of whom, Ho Tzu-hsiao, manages, however, to survive in the body of a newly dead friend (pp. 316 – 23). In 'The Student Tung' (c. 2), a female fox sends Tung to the grave and brings another lover to the verge of death (pp. 133 – 6). In 'Lien-hsiang' (c. 2), we find this dialogue between the she-fox Lien-hsiang and the female ghost Li over the hero's sick-bed in his home in Lini (in Shantung Province) :

Lien-hsiang : I have heard that the female ghost selfishly hastens a man's death, so that, after his decease, she may the more readily cohabit with him. Is this true?

Li :   Not so! There is no pleasure when two ghosts conjugate. If indeed there were pleasure, there is certainly no lack of young male ghosts in the nether world.

Lien-hsiang : The silly girl! If a man indulged in love
with a woman night after night, he would
soon be enfeebled; how much more so
with a ghost!

Li :   But equally an amorous fox can be the
cause of a man's death. What art is it that
you alone possess in being capable of
preserving his health?

Lien-hsiang : You are thinking of creatures that sap the
vitality of men to invigorate their own
constitution. I am not one of those. For
there *are* foxes that do no harm to the
men with whom they come into contact,
but there are *no* ghosts that do no harm
to the men with whom they unite, on
account of their spectral coldness.
(p. 225)

And indeed it is the fox Lien-hsiang that effects the cure of
the hero after his debilitating association with the female
ghost Li. Subsequently Li re-entering life through the body
of the dead daughter of a rich local family, all three are
united (pp. 226–31).

Even apart from their amorous nature, the rivalry between
fox and female ghost is heightened by their nocturnal habits
and the proximity of their dwellings. Ghosts harbour foxes
in their tombs. Ying-ning, a fox mother's daughter, is
brought up in a tomb by the ghost of her stepmother (pp. 155,
158). In 'Ch'iao-niang' (c. 2), the fox mother jealously
guards the prospective son-in-law whom she has restored to
manhood from the attentions of the female ghost Ch'iao-niang,
whose tomb in Kiungshan (on Hainan Island) she and her
daughter San-niang are sharing. The charming competition
between the fox San-niang and the ghost Ch'iao-niang
continues in their roles as model wives to the hero and
exemplary daughters-in-law to his parents (pp. 256–64).
And in 'Ch'ang-t'ing' (c. 10), a male ghost haunts a female

fox, claiming it was no offence against heaven for a ghost to haunt a fox family (p.1334).

Other animal spirits also appear in *Liao-chai chih-i*. A number of tales about dragons (c. 2, pp. 284–5; c. 3, p. 310; c. 4, p. 474; c.7, p.1015) are entirely in the early tradition; two Dragon Kings figure in 'Wan-hsia' (pp.1476–9), and in 'Princess of the West Lake' the Dragon King is away from Tungting Lake (p. 651). Among tales about tigers, 'Hsiang Kao' (c. 6), in which the hero, on changing into a cotton gown given to him by a Taoist in a temple and crouching on all fours, is transformed into a tiger that kills his enemy (pp. 831–3), would seem indebted to the T'ang tale 'The Tiger' (see *supra*, pp. 84–6); other tales about tigers are 'Mr Cat' (c.12, pp.1598–1601) and 'The Stripy Brothers' (c.12, pp.1593–4). There are tales about the turtle, the tortoise, the deer, the wolf, the rat, the frog, lizards, fish, birds, bees and butterflies. Animal spirits known as the 'Five Mighty' (wu-t'ung) that haunt women in Kiangsu and Chekiang provinces, figure in two of the tales (c.10, pp.1417–24; the *wu-t'ung* deities were originally human and widely worshipped in those provinces in the Ming, see T'ien Ju-ch'eng, *Hsi-hu yu-lan chih yü*, Chung-hua ed. 1958, c. 26, pp. 476–7). The monkey disciple of the Buddhist monk Tripitaka appears in one tale (c.11, pp.1459–62), not as an animal spirit, but as a god. And a sprinkling of scholar's fancies such as a horse painted by the Yüan artist Chao Meng-fu that turns into a real horse (c. 8, pp.1027–8) or the brilliant student later discovered to be a huge silverfish (c.10, pp.1349–59), adds to the variety.

What is distinctive of many of the tales is that the spirits clearly manifest their animal characteristics. In 'A-hsien' (c.10), the heroine, a rat spirit, fills the granary with rice (pp.1380–5). In 'Pai Ch'iu-lien' (c. 11), the hero's wife, spirit of a white fish, carries jars of water from her lake in Hupeh to the hero's home in Hopeh in the north, and adds a little of the lake water to her food at each meal, languishing

when the water runs out (pp. 1482 – 8). In 'The Frog God'
(c. 11), the heroine, a frog spirit, increases substantially the
harvest yield but is terrified of snakes (pp. 1464 – 8). And in
'A-ying' (c. 7), a tale about a parrot spirit, Miss Maina, a
mina, sings in the night to the applause of all her bird
companions before having one of her claws bitten off by a
wild animal (pp. 917 – 23).

Though P'u was not uninfluenced by earlier writings, the
tales in *Liao-chai chih-i* are, as he tells us in his Preface,
mainly of folk origin, having been told, in the first instance,
by friends, acquaintances and total strangers in his home or
village, in the library of the Pi family, his employers, at
banquets and gatherings, on journeys by land or by boat, in
inns or under the roofs of his hosts, or supplied by friends and
correspondents in versions he revised and rewrote. This
would account for their refreshing originality. They are not
tied to a narrow moral outlook, nor shaped according to the
demands of Confucian ethics and Buddhist and Taoist moral
teachings; in them, fancy ranges freely, subject only to the
dictates of those great arbiters of Chinese life — chance and
coincidence — and of human nature, the darker side of which
is not glossed over. On the contrary, the wicked, the depraved,
the selfish, the mean and the sordid are revealed in their
pettiness and iniquity without condemnation except in some
ironical comment at the end. And indeed the variety of
human types among P'u's characters, and the often aston-
ishing turn of their speech and behaviour, leading to surprise
developments in the plot, are one great attraction of the tales.

As a narrator also, P'u breaks through conventions and
cliches to concentrate on what matters in the story; literary
precedent, stereotyped expectations and rhetorical embel-
lishment are brushed aside in his concern to convey the
sequence of events in an account of severe economy but with
the most telling effect, harnessing his prose, supple and
concise, in turn artificial and plain, to that end. Over and
above this, he weaves a web of enchantment round the

happenings he recounts, sometimes, as has been noted above, through their settings, so that the reader steps into a magic world, drinking in supernatural experience rather than its ornamental accessories. After even a cursory survey of the supernatural tales of all the preceding ages, the full splendour of P'u's imagination emerges, crowning his magnificent achievement.

Out of 491 tales in *Liao-chai chih-i* I have chosen four — 'The Tou Lass', 'Yellow Pride', 'Yüeh Chung' and 'The Cricket' — which show the art of P'u Sung-ling at its best, though they are not typical examples of his treatment of the supernatural; indeed in sophistication they well exceed the other tales.

I have used the text in the edition of *Liao-chai chih-i* with full collation by Chang Yu-ho (Chung-hua 1962), and *chüan* and page references are to that edition.

1. For Kan Pao's collection of tales 'In search of the Gods', see General Introduction, p. 5, *supra*.
2. An alternative title to the same author's 'In the Land of the Dead and the Living'; see General Introduction, p. 5, *supra*.

'The Tou Lass'

This is the only tale in *Liao-chai chih-i* in which corpses are moved about through supernatural agents. Its theme is nemesis, the closest parallel to it being the T'ang tale alluded to by the author himself in his final comment, Chiang Fang's love story about Huo Hsiao-yü and Li Tenth.

Hsiao-yü, the daughter of a prince by a serving maid, is sixteen, clever and beautiful. Cast out by the family after the prince's death, she becomes a singing girl but hopes to find a talented and handsome husband. The exceedingly gifted Li Tenth, aged twenty and newly arrived at the capital, having been introduced to her by a matchmaker, the two are instantly attracted to each other, and mutually declare their love. That night she expresses her fear that he would cease to love her when her beauty fades, but swearing his eternal devotion, he writes a solemn declaration of his fidelity on a piece of silk. After two years, he is appointed to an office in the provinces; and in the meantime his family has arranged an alliance between him and a cousin. Bowing to his mother's will and ashamed of having broken faith with Hsiao-yü, Li stays away from the girl, who languishes in despair and falls ill. The affair is talked about all over the capital, whither Li presently returns, though keeping himself hidden from Hsiao-yü. A total stranger, clad in a yellow robe, accosts Li in a temple, where he and a few friends are admiring the peonies, and on the pretext of inviting him to his home, brings Li to the house of Hsiao-yü, who rises from her sick-bed to greet Li in silence, and then promises that she will haunt him after her death. Then bursting into a fit of sobbing, she expires. Li marries his cousin but knows no happiness. Once, while in bed, he sees a young man beckoning to his wife from behind the bed-curtains. On another occasion, when his wife is playing on the guitar, a love-knot is thrown through the window on to her lap. He reproaches her, but she refuses to defend herself, and eventually he divorces her. After that, Li is insane with jealousy as far as his womenfolk are concerned. He re-marries twice but with the same consequences ('Huo Hsiao-yü chuan', *T'ang-jen hsiao-shuo*, pp. 77–82).

There is something surrealist about 'The Tou Lass' and indeed it could well have been written in twentieth-century Europe. The tale is in c. 5, pp. 712–15, of the Chang edition of *Liao-chai chih-i*.

The Tou Lass

Nan San-fu, who was descended of a distinguished official's family in Chin-yang (i.e. Taiyuan in Shansi Province), had a villa a dozen or so *li* from his house, being in the habit of riding thither. On one occasion, caught in the rain, he sought shelter in what seemed a spacious cottage in a village along the way. Since the villagers all held Nan in high esteem, the owner of the cottage came out and, stooping low, invited him into a small room, where he sat down, while his host took a broom and swept the floor before offering honey tea. At Nan's insistence, his host also sat down, saying in reply to Nan's inquiry, that his name was Tou T'ing-chang; and before long, the host brought in wine and a tender chicken, and served these up to Nan with extreme deference. The host's daughter, who was of the age to wear a hairpin, busied herself in the kitchen and brought the food to the door of the room, so that only her profile was visible to Nan, who noticed that she was fifteen or sixteen and uncommonly pretty, and was suddenly infatuated.

When the rain stopped, Nan returned to his home and kept thinking of the girl. A few days later he took with him some gifts of grain and cloth to convey his thanks and to further his acquaintance with the family, and from then on became a frequent visitor, often bringing his own wine and food so as to remain the longer. And the girl grew accustomed to the visitor, no longer hiding herself but going about her tasks in his presence. And when Nan looked at her, she would lower her head and smile, causing him to be even more infatuated, so that every two or three days he would visit the Tous.

One day, Farmer Tou happening to be away, Nan sat by himself for a long while before the girl came out to entertain him. Holding her by the arm, Nan tried to caress her, whereupon the girl flushed with shame and sternly resisted him, saying, 'I may be poor but my object is matrimony; and I will not submit to this treatment from a high and mighty gentleman'. At the time Nan had just lost his wife, and making her a bow, said, 'If you deign to honour me with your hand, I shall take no other wife'. The girl then asking Nan to swear that he will marry her, Nan swore by the sun his eternal fidelity, upon which the girl gave her consent. From then on, Nan would wait for Farmer Tou to leave the house before coming to spend his time with the girl, who said imploringly to him, 'These assignations cannot last for ever. My parents would be much honoured if you, who are their patron, would make a formal offer of marriage, to which, I assure you, there would be no impediment. Please hurry!' And Nan promised to do so.

But then considering that a farmer's daughter could not be a fitting match for a man of his consequence, he thought it best to make matrimony a mere excuse to continue his association with the girl. Presently a matchmaker coming along to discuss marriage between Nan and the daughter of a prominent family, after hesitating at first, Nan decided, on hearing that the young lady was beautiful and her fortune great, to allow negotiations to proceed. Meanwhile, the Tou lass finding herself pregnant, became more insistent in her entreaties to him, whereupon Nan stayed away from her altogether. The girl soon giving birth to an infant boy, Farmer Tou was outraged and beat his daughter, who confessed, saying, 'Nan promised on oath to marry me'.

Farmer Tou then sending someone to ask Nan, he denied all knowledge of the affair. And Farmer Tou exposed the infant and again beat his daughter, who secretly asked a woman neighbour to report her sorry plight to Nan, who remained impervious.

The Tou lass then left her own house by night and, finding the exposed infant to be still alive, carried it to Nan's house and knocked on the gate, saying to the door-keeper, 'I only want a word with your master, and if he would but grant me this, I might still live. Though he may have no regard for me, he must have *some* regard for his own son!' The door-keeper reporting this within, Nan commanded that they be kept out of the house. The girl then leaned against the gate and sobbed, her sobbing being heard until the fifth watch; but when the gate was opened in the morning, the Tou lass was found sitting on the step outside the gate, dead, with the infant, also dead, still in her arms.

Filled with indignation, Farmer Tou filed a suit against Nan; and the Magistrate and others all holding Nan to be culpable and deserving of punishment, Nan, being now afraid, offered a bribe of a thousand taels to save himself. The lady with whom marriage negotiations were being made on Nan's behalf then had a dream, in which the Tou lass appeared with her hair all dishevelled, holding an infant in her arms, saying, 'Do not accept the suit of that heartless wretch! If you do, I will kill him'. But the lady's family was attracted by Nan's wealth and eventually agreed to the match.

At the wedding, the trousseau was magnificent; but the bride, though of flawless beauty, yet seemed to be in a state of deep depression. For she was never seen to be smiling and, in bed, would shed tears and, when asked about the cause, remain silent. A few days later, her parents both came to the house, weeping. When Nan hurriedly invited them in and they set eyes on the bride, they said in great agitation, 'From the road we saw our daughter hanging from a peach tree in the back garden, dead. Who can this be

that now greets us?' The bride heard them and, suddenly
changing colour, collapsed in a heap and died before them;
and on Nan taking a closer look, he found the corpse to be
that of the Tou lass.

Nan now hurrying to the back garden, saw that the bride
was indeed hanging from a tree. When in alarm he sent
word to the Tou family, they opened their daughter's tomb
and found the coffin open and the corpse gone. Thereupon
Farmer Tou, still aggrieved by the former injuries done to
his family, again brought the case to court, but the Magistrate, perplexed by its intricacy, could not arrive at a verdict.
Nan now presenting the Tou family with generous gifts and
entreating them to settle the dispute out of court, and,
moreover, bribing the Magistrate, the case was not proceeded
with.

Nevertheless, from then on, the prestige of the Nan
family began to decline; in addition, on account of the reports
of apparitions and untimely deaths, for several years no
family would enter into an alliance with it, though Nan finally
found a lady willing to marry him in the daughter of the higher
graduate Ts'ao over a hundred *li* away. While preparations
for the wedding were still being made, it was rumoured that
a search was on for ladies to be taken into service in the
Emperor's palace, so that families with daughters already
betrothed often sent them before their time to their husbands.
One day, an old woman came to Nan's gate followed by a
sedan-chair, saying that she was escorting the bride from the
Ts'ao family; then helping her charge into the bedchamber,
she apologized to Nan, saying, 'The search for palace ladies
has begun in our area, and while we regret the lack of
ceremony, at least I have brought your bride safely'. To
Nan's question, 'Why are there no wedding guests?' she
replied, 'They will follow with the trousseau', and departed
in all haste.

Nan looked at his bride and found her pretty. They smiled
to each other. Then lowering her head, the bride toyed with

her belt, her gesture and expression being the exact likeness of the Tou lass, whereupon Nan was overcome with revulsion, though keeping silent. The bride then climbed into bed and, wrapping herself in a quilt, covered her own head, to which Nan paid no attention, regarding this as a whim in one newly wedded. When it was evening and no wedding party from the Ts'ao family had arrived, Nan was assailed by doubt, and lifting the quilt to question his bride, he found her dead. Surprised and shocked, he dispatched someone in great haste to tell the Ts'ao family, who, it transpired, had not sent their daughter. The town now buzzed with talk of a dead bride, which reached a certain higher graduate Yao, who had newly buried his daughter and discovered on the following day that the tomb had been rifled and the body removed; and on coming to Nan's house to look at the corpse, Yao found that it was indeed that of his daughter. As Yao pulled back the quilt, he saw that the body was naked, and, in a fury, filed a suit against Nan. The Magistrate had long disapproved of Nan's repeated escapades: he now found Nan guilty of rifling the tomb and defiling the corpse, and sentenced him to death.

The tattler comments: to seduce a girl and then make an honest woman of her may not be construed an act of virtue. How much worse, then, to swear eternal fidelity and then abandon her! What unfeeling cruelty to allow her to be beaten by her father and to weep in vain outside the gate! No wonder a worse punishment than that of Li Tenth, who was haunted by the ghost of Hsiao-yü, whom he had abandoned, was visited upon him.

'Yellow Pride'

In the section 'Spirits of Flowers and Plants' in *T'ai-p'ing kuang-chi*, c. 416–417, there are three tales about flower-spirits appearing in human guise. In 'Lodger in Kuang-hua Temple' (c. 417), the hero meets in the gallery of a temple in the Ts'u-lai Mountains (south-east of Taian in Shantung Province) a white-robed girl and presents her with his white jade ring. On leaving the temple, the girl disappears after a hundred paces or so. The hero then setting out in search, comes across a white lily with very large flowers among the grass, and digging it up, finds his jade ring embedded in the scales of its bulb (pp. 3394–5). And in 'Su Ch'ang-yüan' (c. 417), on his farm near Soochow (in Kiangsu Province) the hero would meet a ruddy-faced girl dressed in white, to whom he gives a jade ring; but, one day, stooping to admire the unusually shaped white lotus flowers before his railing, he finds his ring enfolded in the petals of one of them (p. 3397).

And in 'Ts'ui Hsüan-wei' (c. 416), the hero is visited in his home in Loyang (in Honan Province) on a clear night in spring by several young ladies and their aunt, who expresses displeasure with one of the nieces. The following night, the young ladies return and ask him to set up a banner to protect them from the wind. He then realises that they are the willow, the plum, the peach and the pomegranate in his garden, and that their aunt is the wind goddess (pp. 3392–3; *T'ang Sung ch'uan-ch'i hsüan*, pp.190–1).

Our tale is one of three in *Liao-chai chih-i* in which the lover of a particular flower is rewarded by the spirit of the flower, the other two being 'Ko-chin' (c.10) and 'Hsiang-yü' (c.11).

In 'Ko-chin', a lover of moutan peonies from Loyang visits Tsaochow (i.e. Hotseh in Shantung Province), famous for its moutan peonies. He lodges in a summer-house in a garden full of these flowers and is so charmed with them that he writes a hundred four-line poems about them. Moved by his devotion, the spirit of a purple peony appears to him in the shape of a beautiful woman and eventually returns to Loyang with him. Her cousin, the spirit of a white peony, also marries the hero's younger brother. The women, who claim to be descended from the Duchess of Tsaochow, each give birth to a son. Three years after his first visit, the hero again goes to Tsaochow and discovers that 'The Duchess of Tsaochow' is the name of a purple moutan peony. He now suspects his wife to be a spirit and, upon returning to Loyang, starts to question her. In a fit of pique, the two women vanish, having first hurled their babies into the garden. The babies, too, vanish, but a few days later shoot up as two moutan peony trees, one growing purple flowers, the other, white flowers (pp.1436–43).

In 'Hsiang-yü', a student staying at a Taoist temple on Lao-shan (north-east of Tsingtao in Shantung Province) is visited by the lovely Hsiang-yü ('Fragrant Jade'), the spirit of a moutan peony over ten feet in height in the temple garden. Subsequently, when the peony is removed to another garden, the student is comforted, in Hsiang-yü's absence, by her companion, Chiang-hsüeh ('Purple Snow'), the spirit of a climbing plant. In the spring, however, the peony starts to grow again and, a year later, produces a single flower, from which Hsiang-yü emerges, to be reunited with the student. After a dozen years the student dies and himself becomes a moutan peony tree in the temple garden (pp.1548–55).

K

As for the lover of chrysanthemums, it was recorded of the poet T'ao Yüan-ming (365–427) that on the ninth day of the ninth month, when it was customary to drink chrysanthemum wine, he sat alone a long while among the chrysanthemums by the side of his house in Ch'ai-sang (south-west of Kiukiang in Kiangsi Province) with no wine to quench his thirst. Presently the prefect Wang Hun, sending some wine, the poet promptly drank it up and was drunk.[1] In one of T'ao's 'Drinking Wine' poems also, the poet plucks chrysanthemums by the eastern fence of his dwelling;[2] and in another poem in the same series, he picks the dew-soaked petals of the chrysanthemum and floats them in his wine cup.[3] Such glimpses of the poet have contributed to a stereotyped picture of T'ao the drunk recluse, who loved chrysanthemums. The T'ang poet Tu Fu (712–70), for example, writes:

> I always lamented the hapless T'ao Yüan-ming,
> Facing his chrysanthemums, wineless, penniless.
> It is now the Double Ninth Festival
> And I, too, must ask for wine on credit.[4]

In our tale, though the brother and sister claim to be descendants of T'ao, they do not really embody traits associated with the chrysanthemum: seclusion, loftiness of character, poetry, longevity. The brother does indeed drink immoderately; but apart from their magical ways with chrysanthemum plants, Yellow Pride and her brother are shining examples of prosaic thrift and industry, and in this respect the reader shares in the disappointment of Ma Tzu-ts'ai. There is also no attempt to link the physical beauty of Yellow Pride to the attributes of the chrysanthemum, as there is in 'Ko-chin' in the description of the spirit of the purple peony:

> . . . he clasped her slender waist and her breath was as fragrant as the epidendrum (p.1438).

... her jade-like skin emitted a warm fragrance, and her breath, and even her sweat, was saturated with a sweet odour (p.1439).

'Yellow Pride' is in c.11, pp.1446–52, of the Chang edition of *Liao-chai chih-i*.

1. See T'ao's biography in *Sung shu*, quoted in *Ching-chieh hsien-sheng chi* (Ssu-pu pei-yao ed.); for T'ao Yüan-ming, see Volume II of this series.
2. *Ching-chieh hsien-sheng chi*, c. 3, p. 16b
3. *Ching-chieh hsien-sheng chi*, c. 3, p. 17b
4. Eleventh poem in 'Renewed Anxiety', *Tu Shao-ling chi hsiang-chu*, c. 20; Wen-hsüeh ku-chi ed., VIII, p. 58.

K*

Yellow Pride

Ma Tzu-ts'ai came from a Peking family who had for generations cultivated chrysanthemums, he himself being completely addicted to them, often travelling hundreds of *li* to purchase the best varieties. On one occasion a visitor from Nanking staying with Ma casually mentioned that his cousin had one or two varieties not seen in the north. At the prospect of acquiring some new varieties, Ma immediately set out with his guest for Nanking, where repeated requests earned for Ma two little shoots, which wrapping with the utmost care, he guarded like a treasure.

On his way back to the north he met a youth riding on a donkey behind a curtained conveyance and Ma fell into conversation with him. The youth, who was graceful in appearance and refined in speech, and who bore himself with easy dignity, said that his name was T'ao, and when he asked what Ma was doing, Ma told him the truth. The youth thereupon said, 'All varieties are equally excellent, depending only on the skill of the gardener.' Ma then bringing up the subject of cultivating chrysanthemums, was delighted with the youth's suggestions and asked where he was going. T'ao replied, 'My eldest sister is tired of Nanking, and is looking for a house north of the Yellow River.' Ma then said, 'Poor as I am, my cottage is at your disposal; and if you do not mind its state of dilapidation, you need look

nowhere else.' When T'ao went before the vehicle to tell his
sister, she lifted a curtain, inadvertently showing herself to
be a young woman of twenty or so, of startling beauty, and
said to him, 'As for the house, we wish for nothing grand,
but we do require a large courtyard.' Upon which Ma
answered that he was able to provide this, and thus they
travelled to Peking together.

To the south of Ma's house was a neglected vegetable
garden with a suite of three or four small rooms, and
these being to T'ao's liking, he decided to live there,
coming over every day to the main house in the northern
courtyard to tend Ma's chrysanthemums. T'ao would pull
up a withered plant by the root, replant it and give it a
new lease of life. Now T'ao was very poor; for he fed daily
with Ma, and he and his sister seemed not to do any cooking,
and Mrs Ma, who grew fond of T'ao's sister, often supplied
her with rice by the peck. The sister, whose name was
Yellow Pride, and who had a ready fund of conversation,
would often bring her sewing or help Mrs Ma with the
spinning.

One day T'ao said to Ma, 'Taking advantage of your
kindness, I daily enjoy hospitality from you, who are not a
rich man yourself. This cannot go on for ever, and I propose
to make a livelihood by selling chrysanthemums.' Ma, ever
aloof and disdainful of the crowd, heard T'ao with disgust,
observing, 'I thought you were a recluse above worldly
considerations, and content with poverty. If you do what you
propose, you would be converting your hermitage into a
bazaar and a shame to your chrysanthemums.' T'ao replied,
laughing; 'He is not covetous who lives by his own exertions;
nor can he be considered vulgar who sells flowers as his
occupation. Though the pursuit of wealth is far from
admirable, there is little merit in the pursuit of poverty.'
Ma not deigning to contradict him, T'ao rose and left.
From then on, T'ao would pick up all the weak and
inferior plants rejected by Ma, but he no longer had his

meals with Ma, nor stayed the night in the house, and came only when actually invited.

Before long, it was the chrysanthemum season. Crowds gathered outside T'ao's house, and the place was as noisy and busy as the market. Out of curiosity Ma went across the courtyard and took a look, and saw that the street was filled with people and carts loaded with chrysanthemums, the flowers all being varieties he had not seen before. Despising T'ao for his enterprise and annoyed that T'ao had withheld so many new varieties of chrysanthemums from him, Ma was inclined to cut T'ao dead, and knocked on T'ao's door, intending to rebuke him. T'ao came out and, holding Ma warmly by the hand, dragged him into the southern part of his own estate.

The neglected vegetable garden had been converted into rows of beds of chrysanthemums, not a single patch of ground outside the few rooms but was utilized : the flowers and buds were all perfect, and fresh shoots planted where plants had been newly removed. On scrutinizing the chrysanthemums, Ma realized that they were only varieties which he himself had rejected and thrown away. T'ao took out wine and food from the house, laying them out on a table beside the flower beds, saying, 'Unable to embrace the vow of poverty, I am fortunate in that the last day or two have brought returns that enable me to treat my friend.' Presently a voice from inside the house calling out—'Brother', T'ao went in and brought out some delicious dishes, whereupon Ma asked, 'Why is your sister not married ?' T'ao replied, 'It is not yet time'. Ma asked, 'When will it be time ?' T'ao said, 'In two score and three months'. Ma then asking, 'How so ?' T'ao smiling gave no reply. Thus they caroused and parted good friends as before.

A day or two later, Ma again called, and noticing with increasing wonder that the new shoots were already over a foot in height, demanded to know the secret of their sudden growth. T'ao replied, 'It cannot be explained in words.

Anyhow you who are not dependent on chrysanthemums for your living, do not need to know.' Soon the season being over, T'ao's nursery became quiet again. T'ao then wrapped up his chrysanthemums in rush mats, and had them removed in several carts, with which he himself also departed. Half way through the spring in the following year, T'ao returned with many rare specimens from the south. He set up a stall in the city, and in ten days had sold all his flowers, when he came back to the house to cultivate his chrysanthemums. Many who had bought flowers from T'ao the previous year came again to buy from him; for, though they had kept the root of the plant, by spring it was no longer wholesome. And so T'ao grew richer with each day, and within a year had added an extension to his suite of rooms, and within two years had had a mansion built, all to his own design without his bothering to consult his host. The flower beds having gradually all become part of his house, he bought an adjoining field, and building a wall round it, used it to plant chrysanthemums. In the autumn, he again brought his flowers with him to the south, but this time failed to return in spring.

In the meantime, Mrs Ma fell ill and died. When Ma, who hoped to marry Yellow Pride, sent someone to speak to her on his behalf, Yellow Pride smiled, showing that she was not averse to the proposal, but said that she would wait for her brother's return before deciding. But T'ao was away a whole year and more. In his absence, Yellow Pride superintended the servants in growing chrysanthemums, investing the profits they brought in other ventures. Soon she owned outlying fields to the extent of two thousand *mou*, and their residence had become almost palatial.

One day, a traveller from Eastern Kwangtung brought a letter from T'ao, and when Ma opened it, its message was that Yellow Pride should marry Ma; and when Ma looked at the date, it was the very day of Mrs Ma's decease. Ma then recalled that it was exactly forty-three months previously that he had had the conversation with T'ao in the garden, and marvelled even more. And he sent the letter to Yellow Pride with the question—'Where should the betrothal gifts be sent?' Yellow Pride declined the gifts but accepted the proposal, expressing the wish that Ma leave his old house and live with her; but Ma insisted on living in the old house in the northern courtyard. And a propitious day was chosen and the wedding took place.

Having moved into Ma's house, Yellow Pride had a door made that communicated with her own house, going across every day to supervise her servants at their tasks. Ma, ashamed to be overborne by a rich wife, constantly asked Yellow Pride to have separate inventories made and separate accounts kept for the two house-holds, but Yellow Pride taking all that was necessary from her own house, within half a year Ma's house was filled with her furniture and other movable possessions. After Ma had had them sent back with the injunction that they be not taken again, within ten days sundry pieces had once more found their way into his house. And many times over, with the same results did Ma return all the various things to the other house before Yellow Pride said, 'You *are* kept busy, shining example of incorruptibility!' Whereupon Ma, shamed into silence, no longer insisted on having two separate households, but left all matters to Yellow Pride, who, overruling Ma's objections, proceeded to enlarge his house; and after the builders had been at work for several months, the two houses were joined together, and there was no line of demarcation between them.

But, acceding to his wishes, she no longer sold chrysanthemums; for they now lived more luxuriously than even the best families. Nevertheless, Ma, who had his scruples, said, 'My thirty years of honest poverty has been contaminated by you. Now that I live and breathe, tied to your apron strings, what is left of my manliness? While the world at large prays for riches, I alone pray for poverty.' Yellow Pride said in reply, 'It is not that I am given to covetousness, but without some material possessions we shall incur the censure of men, who will say, 'Poor T'ao Yüan-ming was so destitute that even a hundred generations later his descendants are still in want', and I have to uphold the family honour. Besides, for the poor to become rich is more difficult than for the rich to become poor. Pray feel free to squander all the money there is in the house; I shall certainly not grudge it.' Ma said, 'To squander the money of another is dishonourable.' Yellow Pride then said, 'You cannot abide riches and I cannot abide poverty. There is no help for it but that we maintain separate establishments, so that the pure be not defiled by the unclean.' And so she had a thatched cottage built in the garden for Ma to live in, attended on by a good-looking servant girl, and for a few days Ma felt more at ease; but then he began to long for Yellow Pride, and since she would not go to him, he had to come to her, spending every other night with her in the house. Yellow Pride then laughed, saying, 'I see—the honest poor feeds in one house and sleeps in another. What wonderful nicety!' At which Ma burst out laughing as well and, for want of an apt reply, moved back into the house.

It then happened that Ma had to go to Nanking. It being autumn and the chrysanthemum in season, Ma passed one morning a florist's shop, where pots of perfectly shaped chrysanthemums were laid out, all of the most unusual varieties. Struck by the flowers, Ma suspected them to have been grown by T'ao, and a few moments later, when the owner came out, it was indeed T'ao. After greeting each other in great delight, they gave each other the news, Ma then staying with T'ao. Ma now asked T'ao to return to Peking with himself. T'ao said, 'Nanking is my home town, where I plan to get married and settle. I have accumulated some capital, and shall be grateful if you will hand it over to my sister. At the end of the year I shall visit you both.' But Ma would not hear of it, and again urged T'ao to return with him, adding: 'There is enough in the house for us all to enjoy, and you need not engage in trade again.' And Ma took matters into his own hands and ordered a servant to sell the flowers cheaply, so that in a few days the entire stock was gone. Ma then made T'ao pack his bags, and engaging a boat, they travelled to the north.

When they reached the house, Yellow Pride had already prepared a bed and a suite of rooms for her brother as if she had known in advance of his coming. And as soon as T'ao had unpacked, he directed the servants to work in the garden, to add to its pavilions and arbours, and generally to improve its appearance. Every day he drank and played chess with Ma, not deigning to make other friends, and when Ma sought to find him a wife, T'ao declined the proposal, whereupon Yellow Pride sent two maidservants to attend on him, and after three or four years one of them gave birth to a daughter.

Though T'ao was a deep drinker, he was never seen to be drunk. A friend of Ma's, one Tseng, who also drank heavily, happening once to call, Ma made him engage in a drinking bout with T'ao. Giving rein to their capacity, the two contestants drank with abandon from the morning to the fourth watch of the night, when each had taken a hundred flagons. Tseng, who was dead drunk, lay asleep amid the drinking vessels, while T'ao rose to go to bed but suddenly fell on a bed of chrysanthemums on leaving the house. Then casting aside his clothes, he was transformed into a chrysanthemum plant as tall as a man, with a dozen or so flowers each larger than a man's fist. Startled beyond measure, Ma woke up Yellow Pride, who, hurrying to the plant, pulled it up and laid it flat on the ground, exclaiming in dismay, 'Why is he so drunk?' Then covering the plant with T'ao's clothes, she asked Ma to retire with her and not to watch over it. When at dawn Ma went to the spot, he found T'ao sleeping by the flower bed, and only then realized that both brother and sister were spirits of the chrysanthemum, after which he loved and respected them all the more.

After T'ao had revealed his true identity, he drank even more freely, and would often invite Tseng, who became a boon companion. On the day of the Festival of Flowers in the second month, Tseng called with two servants carrying a large jar of medicated white wine, and he and T'ao agreed to finish it together. They drank till the jar was nearly empty and were still not yet intoxicated, whereupon Ma secretly added a large jugful of wine, which they also drank up. Tseng being now blind drunk, was carried away by his servants, while T'ao, stretched out on the ground, was again turned into a chrysanthemum plant. Ma, no longer surprised, pulled it up as Yellow Pride had done, and then stood beside it to watch it change shape. After a long time, the leaves shrivelled, and being suddenly afraid, Ma only then told Yellow Pride, who cried in a panic, 'You have killed my brother!' And rushing to the plant, she found that the root was dead. And she wailed with grief, and plucked part of the stalk and buried it in a pot, which she kept in her room and watered daily. Ma was filled with remorse, and nursed a deep hatred for Tseng, but learned a few days later that Tseng had died of drunkenness.

But the potted plant flourished, putting forth buds at first and then, in the ninth month, white flowers on short stalks, smelling faintly of wine; and they named it 'The drunk T'ao', and when wine was poured over it, the plant throve. T'ao's daughter later grew up and married into an old and distinguished family; and Yellow Pride ended her days in old age. And there were no further miracles.

The tattler comments : to die of drunkenness after spending a carefree life, though deplored by the world, need not be an unhappy ending. As for the resulting variety of chrysanthemum, it would, if planted in one's garden, be like a friend or the visage of a beautiful woman, well worth the seeking and the cultivation.

'Yüeh Chung'

This is one of the very few truly religious tales in *Liao-chai chih-i*. On the surface it is about the filial piety of a glutton, but the hero's filial piety leads him to true piety, and his gluttony and drunkenness bring about his eventual enlightenment. When his mother was gravely ill, Yüeh Chung cut off a piece of his own flesh, cooked and fed her with it in the hope of curing her. (The belief in the efficacy of this remedy dates back to the T'ang dynasty.) But such was her subsequent revulsion that the intended cure had the contrary effect of hastening her death, after which she became identified in his mind, by stages, with the Bodhisatva Kuan-yin. First, he burnt the image of Buddha on the shrine and set up in its place his mother's tablet, which he worshipped. Next, she came to him while he was ill and in a delirious state, comforting and healing him, and claiming to dwell in the South Sea, the abode of Kuan-yin. Then he joined a group who were going on a pilgrimage to the South Sea. Finally, when, at their destination, he bowed down to worship Kuan-yin, in place of the Bodhisatva, his mother appeared to him in a miracle: she was every one of hundreds of figures each seated on a lotus in the sea. But he was not yet enlightened, and in his quest for the true way, he found a fellow pilgrim in his wife Agate, a former courtesan and an extremely attractive woman, with whom he lived in monastic celibacy.

It was while he was drunk that the vision of Agate clothed in her gorgeous raiments led to his enlightenment.

For Kuan-yin, apart from all her other divine attributes, is the embodiment of filial piety as well as the goddess of motherhood. Kuan-yin, as the princess Miao-shan, gouged out her own eyes and cut off both her arms to be used as ingredients for the medicine by which her ailing father King Chuang was cured,[1] and thus serves as an example of filial piety to all her followers. Being also the patron and protector of mothers, she is sometimes represented as carrying a male infant in her arms. In our tale, for Yüeh Chung's piety, he was rewarded with a son from a previous marriage, an heir to the family.

The South Sea, where Kuan-yin dwelt, was the island of Puto-shan, one of the Chusan Islands off the north-eastern coast of Chekiang Province. The worship of Kuan-yin on Puto-shan had begun in the ninth century,[2] and in 1689, following a period in which the place had been devastated by pirates, the Emperor K'ang-hsi made a benefaction for the rebuilding of the temples and there was consequently a revival of popular interest in the holy island,[3] even though our tale was probably written before then, the author betraying rather vague notions about the whereabouts of Kuan-yin's 'South Sea', mistaking it for the South China Sea. Puto-shan is about two miles to the east of the main island, Chusan, and the portion of the sea between Chusan and Puto-Shan, known as the 'Lotus Sea' (Lien-hua yang), was the scene of several recorded miracles, in which the sea was covered with thousands of lotuses, the flower of Buddhism.[4] On Puto-shan itself were caves in which the Bodhisatva would sometimes appear to the pious. About one of them, Ch'ao-yin Cave, an eye-witness account written by a British sinologue in 1913 reads :

> . . . at certain times, when atmospheric and tidal conditions are favourable, a shaft of sunlight streams into the cave through a gap in the roof called the

t'ien-ch'uang, or 'heaven's window', and strikes athwart the flying foam. The cave then seems to be filled with a tremulous haze, in which the unbeliever sees nothing but sunlit spray, but which to the devout worshipper is a luminous veil through which the '(Bodhisatva) of Love and Pity' becomes visible to the eyes of her faithful suppliants.

Close by the cave stand two little temples, the *Lohantien* or 'Hall of Arahants' and the *Ch'ao-yin-tung-tien*, or 'Hall of the Cave of the Tidal-waves'. A little stone image, one or two empty shrines and incense-jars, an iron-railing, and a rock bearing the inscription *Hsienshen-ch'u*, indicate the spot from which the visitor is invited to gaze into the so-called cave. This spot is known as the *Ch'iu-hsien-t'ai*—the terrace whereon the pilgrim kneels and prays.[5]

'Yüeh Chung' is in c.11, pp.1540–7, of the Chang edition of *Liao-chai chih-i*.

1. See G. Dudbridge, *The Legend of Miao-shan*, 1978, pp. 25–34, for early versions of the story.
2. R. F. Johnston, *Buddhist China*, 1913, pp. 293–4; *P'u-t'o lo-chia hsin-chih*, facsimile of edition of 1931, Taipci 1971, c. 3, p. 2a.
3. Johnston, pp. 348–54; *P'u-t'o lo-chia hsin-chih*, c. 4, p. 6a.
4. Johnston, pp. 322–4; *P'u-t'o lo-chia hsin-chih*, c. 2, pp. 25a–b and c. 3, p. 5a, p. 6a.
5. Johnston, pp. 299–300.

Yüeh Chung

Yüeh Chung was a native of Sian (in Shensi Province), born posthumously after his father's early death. Chung's mother was a devout Buddhist who abstained from flesh food and alcoholic drinks, but when Chung grew up, he became inordinately fond of wine and meat, disapproving in his heart of his mother's ascetic ways and, every now and then, offering her choice dishes for which she loudly reprimanded him. Later, when his mother fell ill and seemed on the point of death, she suddenly longed for meat, which being unable to obtain there and then, he cut off some flesh from his left hip and cooked it, and offered it to her. When she was in some measure recovered, regretting that she had broken her vow, she starved herself to death. Chung was disconsolate, and took a sharp knife and cut off a chunk of the flesh from his right hip, the knife penetrating to the hip bone. But he was saved by members of his household, who applied a healing ointment to the wound and bandaged it, so that he recovered. And remembering the chastity of his mother as a widow and pitying her blind faith, he burnt the image of Buddha on the shrine and set up in its place a tablet to his mother, which he regularly worshipped. And whenever he was drunk, he would weep before the tablet.

At the age of twenty, Chung, who until then had been a virgin, married, but three days after the wedding, declared

that intercourse between man and woman was the very
height of indecency, which he would not indulge in, and sent
his wife back to her home. His father-in-law Ku Wen-yüan
sent relatives three or four times to intercede with Chung,
who remaining adamant, Ku married his daughter several
months later to someone else. From then on, Chung led the
life of a bachelor for ten years, becoming even more un-
conventional in his ways, drinking in taverns in the company
of actors and domestic servants and, if people in the vicinity
came with requests for assistance, readily obliging them.
On one occasion, when someone about to marry off his
daughter said that she had no stew-pan, Chung took the one
on his own stove and gave it to the man, so that a stew-pan
had to be borrowed from a neighbour for cooking his next
meal. And the rabble taking advantage of Chung's good
nature, swindled him day and night. Once, a gambler short
of funds pretended that he was hard pressed by tax-gatherers
and that he was about to sell his son to satisfy their demands,
whereupon Chung, who had set aside a sum of money for
the payment of his own taxes, gave it to the man. Then,
when the tax-gatherers came to the door, Chung had to resort
to a pawnbroker to raise the required sum. In this way
Chung's fortune daily diminished.

When, in earlier days, Chung was still prosperous, his
clansmen were wont to visit him, taking from his house
whatever they fancied without his being much concerned;
but when he grew poor, they no longer came to the house,
and he regarded this with indifference. It chanced that Chung
was ill on his mother's anniversary day and unable to visit
her grave, and sending a servant to ask his clansmen to
sacrifice at the grave on his behalf, met with excuses and
refusals. Pouring a libation before his mother's tablet, Chung
wailed with grief; and much troubled by the thought that he
himself had no heir, he felt his condition worsen. In his state
of delirium he felt someone caress him, and when he half
opened his eyes, saw that it was his mother. He asked her in

wonder, 'Why have you come?' She replied, 'Since there was no one at the grave, I have returned to the house to partake of the offerings and attend to your illness'. He then asked, 'Where do you dwell, mother?' And she said, 'In the South Sea'. When she had finished massaging him, he felt suddenly refreshed, and opening his eyes wide and looking round him, could see no one; but his illness was cured.

When Chung was well again, he thought of making a pilgrimage to the South Sea. A fellowship having been formed in the next village for the purpose of going on such a pilgrimage, Chung sold ten *mou* of his fields to raise the necessary funds and asked to join in; but members of the fellowship, who considered him a glutton, refused to accept him, though eventually allowing him to travel in their company. On the way, Chung continuing to drink wine and feed on beef and shallots and garlic, so that he reeked of uncleanness, the other pilgrims, who were shocked by him, gave way to their abhorrence and left one day when Chung was drunk and asleep, after which Chung travelled by himself. When he reached Fukien Province, a friend inviting him to drink, a celebrated courtesan in the company whose name was Agate offered to accompany him when Chung said that he was on a pilgrimage to the South Sea. Accepting the offer with delight, Chung waited for her to pack before setting out again, eating and sleeping with her, though remaining chaste.

When they reached the South Sea, members of the fellowship laughed scornfully to see Chung with a courtesan and would not worship in their company; sensing this, Chung and Agate let the others precede them in the ceremony. And when the others bowed down, they saw no vision, but when Chung and Agate prostrated themselves, the sea was covered by lotus flowers visible to all, with on each flower a seated figure adorned with a string of beads, each figure being for Agate a Bodhisatva, and for Chung his mother. Calling out 'Mother' and rushing towards the flowers, Chung leapt into the sea. The lotus flowers now turned into coloured clouds, covering the sea like a tapestry and vanishing before long to reveal the clear, undulating waves, while Chung found himself unaccountably on the shore, his clothes and shoes quite dry. Still gazing at the sea, Chung cried his heart out, the sound of his wailing reverberating among the adjoining islands; but Agate gently restrained him, and they left the temple in grief, and taking a boat, headed for the north.

In Fukien, Agate having been invited by an important family to entertain their guests, Chung, while staying by himself at the inn, came across a boy aged eight or nine begging for food in the market. The boy, who did not seem to be a street urchin, said, when Chung questioned him, that he had been driven out by his step-mother. Taking pity on the child, who now clung to him, appealing for help, Chung took it back with him to the inn. And, when he asked the child what its name was, it gave this reply: 'My name is A-hsin, my surname Yung. My mother, who was from the Ku family, told me it was six months after her marrying into the Yung family that I was born, and that my real surname is Yüeh'. Much startled, Chung considered that, though he did consummate his marriage, one brief encounter should not have given rise to offspring. So he eagerly asked, 'Yüeh of which district?' The boy replied, 'I do not know. But my mother gave me a letter to keep when she was dying, and warned me not to lose it'. Chung then demanding at once to see the letter, discovered it to be the certificate of divorce he himself had written for his bride of the Ku family. And he cried in amazement, 'So you are my son!' The age of the boy agreeing with the certificate, Chung was satisfied that he had really found his son and was much comforted.

But Chung was without a livelihood, and after two years, with his land nearly all sold, he could no longer afford to keep servants. When, one day, father and son were cooking a meal, in walked a beautiful woman, who was none other than Agate. When Chung asked in surprise why she had come,

Agate said smiling, 'Is that not obvious? After all, we have cohabited. I could not have followed you home earlier because of my obligation to my foster-mother. Now that she is dead, if I do not marry, I shall be without protection, and if I marry a rake, I shall be without self-respect. My only course, then, is to marry *you*, and I have come thousands of *li* to join you'. And laying down her bundles, she attended to the cooking. And Chung was greatly pleased.

That night, father and son slept together as before, while Agate was housed in another room. And Agate took good care of A-hsin, who treated her like a mother. When the relatives and neighbours heard about Agate's coming, they feasted and congratulated Chung, and Chung and Agate were both gratified. And when visitors came, Agate provided for their entertainment without Chung's bothering to ask where the food and drink had come from. And Agate took some of her gold and pearls, and redeemed, with these, Chung's property; and she bought servants as well as cattle and horses, so that theirs became once again a flourishing household.

Chung would often say to Agate, 'When I am drunk, you must keep out of my way and not let me see you'. To which Agate would agree, smiling. Then, one day, when Chung was thoroughly drunk, he hastily summoned Agate, who appeared before him in her most gorgeous raiments. After gazing at her a long while, Chung suddenly burst into raptures, dancing with joy and crying aloud, 'Enlightened! I am enlightened!' And becoming instantly sober, he saw the world bathed in light and his own abode transformed into the gleaming towers and halls of a jade palace in heaven, the vision lasting a full hour or so. From that time on, no longer frequenting the taverns, he only drank at home in Agate's presence, while she fed on vegetarian dishes and sipped tea.

One day, being mildly intoxicated, Chung asked Agate to inspect the old wounds on his hips; and finding that they were in the shape of two red lotus buds rising from his flesh, she wondered at them. Chung said, smiling, 'When the buds flower, our mock marriage of twenty years comes to an end'. And Agate heard, and believed, him. Then, when they took a wife for A-hsin, Agate gradually left household affairs to her daughter-in-law, and lived with Chung in another court-yard, where A-hsin and his wife attended on them once every three days, not otherwise troubling the parents except when in real difficulty. And Agate kept two servant girls only, one to warm the wine, the other to make the tea.

Then, one day, after A-hsin and his wife had given Agate a long report on household matters in their part of the house, they all went to see Chung, whom they found sitting on his couch with his feet bare. As soon as Chung heard them coming, he opened his eyes and, smiling, said, 'How very fortunate! I knew that you would all come', after which he shut his eyes again. Agate asking in alarm, 'What are you going to do?', looked at his wounds and saw that there was a blooming lotus on each hip; then trying his breath, she found that he had expired. With her hands she firmly closed the petals of each lotus, saying, 'Braving difficulties, I came thousands of *li* to marry you; and I went to some trouble to teach your son and train your daughter-in-law. Since I only have two or three more years, why do you not wait for me?' And after some time, Chung suddenly opened his eyes and said smiling, 'Since you have your own mundane affairs to see to, why will you have me accompany you? So be it then; I will stay for your sake'. Letting go her hands, Agate found that each lotus flower was again a bud. And Chung lived on, talking and laughing as before.

Over three years later, Agate, who was nearly forty but who looked twenty, suddenly said to Chung, 'It is most unbecoming for one's corpse, when dead, to be bandied about by undertakers'. She then ordered two coffins to be made, and when A-hsin asked in dismay what she intended to do with them, replied, 'That is beyond your knowledge'. When the coffins were ready, Agate bathed and adorned herself, saying to A-hsin and his wife, 'I am about to die'. A-hsin said weeping, 'These many years we have not known want under your wise management of our household. And now, before you have enjoyed the fruits of your toil, why do you talk of leaving us?' Agate said, 'The son reaps what the father has sowed. The servants and cattle and horses are what your father's former debtors owed him, and have nothing to do with me. An attendant strewing the flowers in the Queen of Heaven's procession, I was banished, for having allowed my thoughts to stray to earthly things, to this world for thirty odd years, but now my period of exile is at an end'. And she climbed into the coffin and, when they called her, her eyelids were shut. Weeping aloud, A-hsin went to tell his father, to find him also in full dress but dead. Thereupon, howling with grief, A-hsin put his father's body in the other coffin, and had both coffins placed in the hall, but put off funeral ceremonies for several days in the hope that they might revive. And a light emanated from the region of Chung's hips which lit up the walls, while a fragrant mist from Agate's coffin seeped into the neighbouring courtyards; but when the lids of the coffins were nailed down, the light and the fragrance grew faint.

As soon as the funeral was over, the Yüeh clan, coveting Chung's wealth, conspired to dispossess A-hsin on the ground that he was not Chung's son, taking the case to court. The Magistrate, unable to decide the issue, proposed giving half of Chung's estate to the Yüeh clan. A-hsin then appealing to a higher court, the case dragged on.

In the beginning, when Chung sent his bride home, her father Ku married her to one Yung, who migrating soon afterwards to Fukien Province, was not heard from again. Ku being old and without an heir, and longing all the more for his daughter, set out for Fukien in search of his son-in-law, only to learn that his daughter had died and that her son had been turned out of doors, whereupon he complained to the local Magistrate. The son-in-law Yung, being afraid, tried

L

to appease Ku by offering him a sum of money, which Ku refused to accept, insisting instead on having his grandson, whom Yung and Ku sought all over the Prefecture without success.

One day, as Ku was on the high road, he saw a decorated sedan-chair coming towards him, and when he stepped aside to keep out of its way, an elegant woman in it called aloud to him, 'Are you not old Mr Ku?' When Ku said that he was, the woman said, 'Your grandson, who is my son, is reunited with the Yüeh family, but in deep trouble. Desist from your lawsuit and hurry at once to him!' Ku seeking to inquire further, the sedan chair flew past. Thereupon, accepting the money from the Yung family, Ku travelled back to Sian, where the case of Chung's estate was causing a stir, and going before the court, gave a full account of the events down to the details of the dates of his daughter's divorce and remarriage, and the birth of his grandson. The case then went against the Yüeh clan, who were driven out of court. United at last with his lost grandson A-hsin, Ku learned, on telling his story, that the time of his encounter with the woman in the sedan-chair had been the very day of Agate's death. And A-hsin moved his grandfather into his own house, where Ku, alotted a suite of rooms, was waited on by a maidservant, by whom he had, at the age of sixty odd, a son, who was well looked after by A-hsin.

The tattler comments: To refrain from wine and meat is but the semblance of Buddha-hood; only childlike simplicity is the reality of Buddha-hood. Yüeh Chung regarding the beautiful courtesan as a fellow pilgrim and not as a connubial partner, they lived together for over a score years, the feeling existing between them being one of attachment as well as detachment, as beseems true followers of Buddha, not comprehensible to the worldly.

'The Cricket'

In the section 'Insects' in *T'ai-p'ing kuang-chi*, c. 473 – c. 479, there are tales in which various insects, including the cicada, the praying mantis, the earthworm, the ant, the spider, the fly, the bee and the mole-cricket, transform themselves into men and women, the ant being a favoured subject. In 'Hsü Hsüan-Chih' (c. 478), hundreds of armed riders from an ant kingdom under the hero's window in his house in Soochow (in Kiangsu Province) stage a hunt by night on his carpet, and a large party attending their red-capped and purple-robed King hold a picnic on the hero's desk and fish in his stone ink-slab (pp. 3936–9). And in 'The Prefect of Nan-k'o' (c. 475), the hero lying drunk on the porch of his house near Yangchow (in Kiangsu Province) is conveyed in his dream by carriage through a hole in a nearby ancient locust tree into a strange land, in which he marries the Princess and governs as Prefect of Nan-k'o for twenty years before being sent home. Upon waking, ordering his servants to dig under the hole in the tree, he comes upon a whole ant kingdom with an adjoining fief, which was the Prefecture of Nan-k'o (pp. 3910–15; *T'ang-jen hsiao-shuo*, pp. 85–90).

As for mole-crickets, in the early tale 'Shih Tzu-jan' (c. 473), the hero superintending the labourers at work on the family field in Lingling (in Hunan Province) is visited in his little hut at night by a man clad in yellow dressed-silk garments calling himself 'Lu Kou' (a transposition of vowels from lou-ku, 'mole-cricket'), who says that he lives by a stream. A few days later the workmen digging up an ant-hill by a ditch, come across a pit full of mole-crickets, several being larger than the rest, and one, a monstrous size, and the hero kills them all by pouring boiling water over them (p. 3898). And in 'Lu Fen' (c. 474), the hero and several of his friends hear laughter and music from a locust tree in the courtyard in his home in Hsia-yang (i.e. Linfen in Shansi Province) and are invited by a maidservant clad in green and black through a hole in the tree into an elegant residence called 'Bower of Prescience of Rain', where they are received by a lady in purple and invited to a banquet attended by seven or eight other beautiful ladies dressed in white or green or yellow. But a strong gust of wind cracks the beam of the Bower and the party breaks up in confusion, the hero and his friends returning later to the courtyard to find that the tree trunk has been torn open by the wind. Lighting a torch, they discover an ants'-nest with three or four mole-crickets and a few earthworms, all dead, in it (pp. 3902−3).

In other tales, the body of a dead woman is transformed into an insect. 'The Silkworm Daughter' (c. 479) records the age-old tradition of the origin of silkworms. A tribal leader in Kwanghan (in Szechwan Province) having been held in captivity for over a year by another tribe, his wife offers their daughter in marriage to whomsoever is able to bring the father home. Thereupon their horse breaks out of the stable and, a few days later, carries the leader home on its back, after which the horse never stops neighing as if laying claim to the hand of the daughter. The father eventually kills the horse and leaves its hide in the courtyard to dry in the sun, but the daughter passing by, the horse hide suddenly wraps itself round her and flies off, being found, ten days later, perched on a mulberry tree, with the body of the daughter transformed into silkworms (pp. 3944−5). (For another version of this tale, see *Sou shen chi*, ed. Hu, c. 14, pp. 104−5).

Our tale, in which the soul of a boy is metamorphosed to an insect while his body lies in a coma, has an antecedent in the T'ang tale 'The Carp' (see *supra*, pp. 71–5), in which the soul of the sick Hsüeh Wei goes swimming and is changed into a fish.

In *Liao-chai chih-i* itself, there is also the tale of 'Chu-ch'ing' (c.11), in which the hero lies almost dead in the temple of a river god (probably at Fu-ch'ih-k'ou along the Yangtze in Hupeh Province, 55 kilometres west of Kiukiang) while his soul is transformed into a crow (pp.1516–17), though the rest of the narrative goes beyond the dimensions of our tale. As a crow, the hero finds a mate in Chu-ch'ing, a crow who later becomes a goddess. When hit by a pellet from a soldier's cross-bow, the hero dies and returns to his human body. Three years later, visiting the same temple, he feeds the crows, solemnly addressing them: 'If Chu-ch'ing be among you, let her stay!' Then, on a further visit, again feeding the crows, he makes the same appeal to Chu-ch'ing. That night Chu-ch'ing appears to him as a young woman and transports him to her home, and when he eventually leaves, she presents him with a suit of black clothes, 'which he had worn as a crow': clad in it, he could fly to her whenever he wished. (pp.1517–20)

And in 'A-pao' (c. 2), the love-crazed Sun Tzu-ch'u's soul reactivates the dead body of a parrot, which thereupon flies to the side of his beloved A-pao, while Sun's body remains inert, though not completely cold (p. 236).

There would seem to be a factual basis to our tale. It is recorded of the Ming Emperor Hsüan-tsung (reign title, Hsüan-te) in Lü Pi's *Ming-ch'ao hsiao-shih*, Hsüan-lan-t'ang ts'ung-shu ed., c.6, pp. 2a–b:

'A horse for a cricket'

The Emperor was passionately fond of cricket fights and would send to the region south of the Yangtze for crickets, which greatly rising in value, fetched prices of over a dozen ounces of silver each. There was an officer responsible for the grain levy in Feng-ch'iao (near Soochow in Kiangsu Province), who, because he had received orders from the Prefect for the requisitioning of crickets, found the very best of them and exchanged his steed for it. His wife and concubine marvelled at the exchange and peeped into the bowl in which the insect was kept, whereupon the cricket escaped. In a fright, the wife hanged herself. When the husband returned and found his wife dead, being disconsolate and also fearing the law, he, too, hanged himself.

'The Cricket' is in c.4, pp. 484–9, of the Chang edition of *Liao-chai chih-i*.

The Cricket

In the Hsüan-te reign (1426–35) cricket fights were the rage in the Palace, so that every year crickets were exacted as part of the levy from the populace. Though in the western regions crickets were uncommon, a certain Magistrate of Hwayin (in Shensi Province) sent one to the Governor to curry favour, and the insect turned out to be a good fighter, whereupon the Magistrate was told to send up crickets regularly. The Magistrate passing the request on to the village headmen, at the market idlers kept the best crickets in cages, selling them at unheard of prices. And in the name of the cricket levy, unscrupulous headmen demanded exorbitant sums from the people, so that the presentation of a single cricket often proved to be the ruin of several families.

There was one Ch'eng Ming, a student unable to pass his degree examination, who, being an old-fashioned person, not given to asserting himself, was enlisted as village headman by the crafty clerks. Try as he might, Ch'eng could not wriggle out of his onerous post, and before a year was out, his meagre fortune was used up. And he then had to deal with the cricket levy. Not daring to extort money from the villagers and not able to afford to pay for a cricket himself, in his desperation he was ready to kill himself. But his wife said, 'What use would your dying be? Would it not be better to look for crickets in the hope of finding a good one?'

Ch'eng agreeing, set out early and returned late each day, carrying a tube of bamboo and a gauze cage to where the grass grew thick amidst tumbledown walls, where he would remove stones and search in holes for crickets, with little success. He did catch two or three, but they were weak and inferior specimens, not up to the stated requirements. Meanwhile the Magistrate set a time limit for the requisitioning of crickets, punishing those who were tardy: Ch'eng was given a hundred strokes of the rod in the space of a dozen days, so that his legs and hips were covered with bleeding wounds, and he was no longer able to move about and catch crickets. As he lay on his bed, he could only think of ending his own life.

Then a hunch-backed witch, who was a fortune-teller, came to the village, and Mrs Ch'eng taking a small sum of money, went to consult her, finding at the gate a crowd of old women and young girls, and, within, a secluded room screened off by a bamboo curtain, in front of which was a small table with an incense burner on it. While the inquirer offered incense and bowed down twice, the witch, who stood on one side, mumbled some gibberish as in prayer, which all heard in awe, and after a little while, from behind the bamboo curtain a piece of paper was thrown out, which satisfied all the inquirer's questions. Placing her money on the table and bowing down as the previous inquirer had done, Mrs Ch'eng received, when after some time the curtain was lifted, a piece of paper containing no words but only a picture: in the centre were some buildings like a temple, and in the background, a mound, at the foot of which were strangely shaped stones and thorns and thick vegetation, amidst which hid a cricket; close by was a frog, which seemed about to leap. Though Mrs Ch'eng was puzzled by the picture, she took note of the cricket, which seemed an answer to her prayers, and folding up the picture carefully, took it home to show Ch'eng.

After studying the picture, Ch'eng said to himself,

'Perhaps it is an indication of where I might find a cricket'; then thinking the scene depicted to be just like Great Buddha Temple to the east of the village, he supported himself with a stick and set off for the temple with the picture. On skirting the old grave-mound behind Great Buddha Temple, he saw, to his amazement, strangely shaped stones resembling those in the picture, whereupon moving slowly, he strained his ears to catch the least noise from among the thick undergrowth. It was like looking for a needle or a mustard seed, every faculty of his being alerted, but before he had found anything, a toad suddenly leapt out. Even more amazed, Ch'eng hurried after it, and when the toad went among the grass, continued to follow it until he suddenly noticed a cricket among the roots of the thorns. When Ch'eng swooped upon the cricket, it went into a hole among the stones and would not come out again when he tried to tickle it with the bearded end of a grass stalk. Ch'eng then filling the hole with water from the bamboo tube, the cricket emerged, a fine and strong specimen, and hurrying after it, he at last caught it. And when he looked at the cricket, it had a large body and a long tail, a green neck and golden wings. Overjoyed, Ch'eng brought it home in the cage, and the whole family congratulated him as if he had dug up a treasure. And Ch'eng kept the cricket in a bowl and fed it on crab's meat and chestnuts, lavishing on it all his attentions before he could deliver it to the Magistrate to fulfil his obligation.

Ch'eng had a nine-year-old son, who, when he saw that his father was away, secretly lifted up the lid of the bowl to look at the cricket. But the insect immediately hopped out, its movements so fast that the boy, jumping up and down the room in pursuit, could hardly keep up with it. When, at last, the boy succeeded in catching it, one of its legs had come off and its belly, too, had cracked open, so that it seemed half-dead. Being seized by fear, the boy, weeping, told his mother what had happened, and when she had heard his account, she turned ashen pale. Rounding on him, she cried, 'Accursed

one! You have brought your own death upon yourself!
When your father comes back, he will quit scores with you!'
And the boy went away sobbing. Ch'eng returning before
long, when he heard what his wife had to say, he became
numb with a sudden chill; then, when he angrily demanded
where his son was, the boy was nowhere to be seen. Presently
they found his body in the well. Anger now turning into
sorrow, they howled over his body, Ch'eng and his wife
each sitting with their face to the wall by their cheerless
hearth, their dinner uncooked, in silent despair. As it was
then late afternoon, they thought they would bury the corpse,
but on touching the body, found that it was still breathing,
and so laid it on the couch. At midnight the boy revived, so
that they were in some measure comforted. Then looking
at the empty cage, Ch'eng thought again of his lost cricket,
and he sighed and choked; but durst not question his son
further. All night long, he did not sleep a wink, and dawn
found him lying stiff on his bed, plunged in deep melancholy.

Suddenly he heard an insect chirping outside his gate.
Ch'eng rose at once. There indeed was a cricket, and he went
after the insect, which would hop after each chirping, with
great speed. When he put his palm over it, it remained so
still as if it were hardly there. When, then, he raised his
palm a little, it hopped and was away again. He again
followed it, when it turned a corner and was lost to his view,
but looking round, he found it perched on the wall—a short
and small cricket, dark red in colour, not the former one.
Finding that it was so small a cricket, Ch'eng still sought
the one that had got away, when suddenly the cricket on
the wall jumped into his sleeve. Ch'eng looked at it again:
it was more like a mole-cricket, square in the head and long
in the legs, with wings that displayed a plum-blossom pattern,
indeed a fine specimen, and he gladly kept it. But he durst
not present it to the Magistrate without some test of its
prowess.

There was a young fellow in the village who kept a cricket

which he named 'Crab-shell Green' and which had defeated all the crickets in the neighbourhood. Expecting a large profit from it, he asked for a fantastic price, which no-one would pay. This young man came to visit Ch'eng, and upon seeing Ch'eng's cricket in its cage, he laughed aloud with his hand over his mouth. The visitor then took out his own cricket and placed it beside Ch'eng's, and Ch'eng finding that it was a large and long cricket, was ashamed of his own small insect and unwilling to risk a fight, which the young man now insisted on, Ch'eng then considering that it was useless to have an inferior cricket and that it would be as well—just for the fun of it—to let the fight take place, they put both insects in the same bowl, the smaller one crouching there, motionless like a piece of wood, which was the cause of further mirth on the part of the young fellow. Even when provoked with hog's bristles, the small cricket remained quite still, which induced the visitor again to laugh; then, after repeated provocation, Ch'eng's cricket rushed forward in a fury and went straight for its opponent, and bristling all over, attacked it savagely, before long springing up, rearing its tail and stretching its antennae, and biting the neck of the large insect. Alarmed, the young man immediately stopped the fight, and the small cricket chirped loudly as if to announce its victory to its master.

Overjoyed, Ch'eng continued to watch his cricket with the young fellow, when suddenly a cock came forward to peck at the insect. Ch'eng shouted out in alarm, but the cock missing its target, the cricket hopped and was a foot away. The cock advancing in pursuit, caught the cricket in one of its claws; and stamping his foot, his countenance altered, Ch'eng thought all was lost, but then saw the cock straining its neck and flapping its wings as if in great distress : the cricket was now perched on the cock's comb, which it was biting with all its might. Ch'eng was highly delighted and overwhelmed with wonder, and catching hold of the cricket, placed it in its cage.

The next day he presented the cricket to the Magistrate, who, disappointed to find such a small insect, angrily reproved Ch'eng, who then described the feats it had performed. The Magistrate, unconvinced, tried it out in fights with other crickets, with Ch'eng's cricket defeating them all. The Magistrate then had a cock to peck at it, and the cricket triumphed over the cock in the manner Ch'eng had described. Thereupon rewarding Ch'eng, the Magistrate presented the cricket to the Governor. And the Governor was gratified, and sent the cricket in a gold cage to the Emperor with an account of its merits. Ch'eng's cricket having been consigned to the Chamberlain in the Palace, crickets presented from all over the empire, including such doughty fighters as 'Butterfly', 'Praying Mantis', 'Oilskin' and 'Stripy Forehead' were tried out in contests with it, in which it triumphed over them all; it would, moreover, dance to the sound of music, thus making it even more of a prodigy. And the Emperor was graciously pleased, and bestowed gifts of horses and silks on the Governor. And the Governor remembered the Magistrate, who before long was recommended as 'meritorious'. And the Magistrate freed Ch'eng of his obligations as village head-man, and recommended to the Chief Examiner that Ch'eng be made a member of the local College of graduates.

Over a year later, Ch'eng's son, who had lain in a coma, suddenly regained his health and spirits, saying, 'I was transformed into a cricket, an excellent fighter, and it is only now that I have returned to myself'. And the Governor also munificently rewarding Ch'eng, within a few years his property had become vastly enlarged and included ten thousand *mou* of fields, a mansion of many towers and pavilions, and hundreds of cattle and sheep, the procession of horses accompanying him when he went out of the house far exceeding that of the old and distinguished families.

The tattler comments : when by chance the Emperor makes use of an object, the occasion being over, it is promptly erased from the royal memory; but those in attendance will make it into a precedent, to be followed at all times, and what with the greed and rapacity of officials, the matter will have no rest until hundreds of people have been compelled to sell their wives and children. Therefore, every single step of the Emperor's concerns the populace and may not be lightly taken. Ch'eng Ming was reduced to poverty by bad officials but elevated to wealth and pomp by a cricket. When, as village headman, he was beaten by the Magistrate, could he have known that he would become so rich? To reward a good man, heaven sees fit to raise also the Governor and the Magistrate; thus the saying — 'When a pious man rises to heaven, his chickens and dogs follow him' — is borne out by our tale.

DATE DUE

PRINTED IN U.S.A.